Starting Mountaineering
and Rock Climbing

Donald Law

Photographs by John Clements

DAVID & CHARLES

Newton Abbot London North Pomfret (VT) Vancouver

Dedicated to
Franz Weimer and Carsten Kroghsbo
who saved my life

© Donald Law 1977
ISBN 0 7153 7322 6
Library of Congress Catalog Card Number
76-54078

Set in 11 on 12pt Bembo
and printed in Great Britain
by Biddles Ltd, Guildford
for David & Charles (Publishers) Limited
Brunel House   Newton Abbot   Devon

Published in the United States of America
by David & Charles Inc
North Pomfret   Vermont 05053   USA

Published in Canada
by Douglas David & Charles Limited
1875 Welch Street North Vancouver BC

Contents

		page
1	About Mountains and Mountaineering	7
2	Before You Begin	13
3	What to Wear and Carry	22
4	Hillwalking	38
5	Scrambling and Climbing	51
6	Rock Climbing	58
7	Rope	73
8	Other Equipment	90
9	Winter Climbing	101
10	First Aid and Serious Emergencies	112
	Glossary of Welsh Names	125
	Glossary of Scottish Names	130
	Appendices:	
	1 The Alpine Scene	133
	2 Mountain Photography	137
	Bibliography	141

1 About Mountains and Mountaineering

Mountains beckon us. They are true adventure, developing our courage, endurance, patience and presence of mind. Geoff Winthrop, mountaineer and author, declared: 'In climbing mountains danger is a constant element . . . it is always with us, behind the veil of pleasant circumstances, and it can be upon us before we are aware.'

The simplest climb can be made perilous by unforeseen weather changes, faulty footwear, rope, or other equipment, and a good climber checks his equipment before each ascent. An unprepared person could perish on an easy hillwalk – it needs only a sprained ankle when you are alone, then a sudden heavy drop in temperature, an evening and night in severe cold without adequate clothing, and exposure and even death might follow.

This book tells you how to avoid such discomforts and dangers, and how to make the four distinct forms of climbing – hillwalking, scrambling, climbing and rock climbing – as safe as possible, as well as interesting and exciting. It shows the way to avoid wasteful and dangerous errors, explains how well trained people who know what to do can survive terrible conditions, spend a night on a wind-withered ridge, or a couple of days stranded in some snow-hole bivouac, and come away from the experience safely, barely aware of any discomfort.

Hazlitt implied that by going on a journey we escape from ourselves. I believe that through mountaineering in any form we find ourselves. No one ever forgets the excitement of their first climb. Mountaineering teaches us to take calculated risks, while carefully assessing the degree of hazard we accept The presence of danger is one of the attractions, the man who has never encountered fear can never know his own courage. In *The Ascent of F6* Auden and Isherwood described a haunted mountain upon which every climber encountered whatever he feared most. I firmly believe that mountaineering can help us overcome whatever fears we have in life. The mountains teach us to recognise hazards, weigh them against knowledge and experience, and make calm decisions. The rewards justify all efforts and dangers.

The mountains we climb were there before the Egyptians built the pyramids, and when our skyscrapers and subways all turn to dust, they will still be there. Men have only been climbing, however, for a relatively short time, and frequently mountains were objects of fear and superstition for early generations, some being said to be the abode of the gods – one known as Meru was reputed to be 80,000 leagues high! Some heights in Greece acquired a reputation for sanctity, and the Himalayas ('the abode of snows') are still regarded by many as altitudes to which one may go to think, learn and gain wisdom.

The Roman emperor Trajan climbed Etna to watch the sunrise, and in the nineteenth century Lafcadio Hearn recorded the Japanese of his day ascending a mountain to sit upon its slopes and watch the sunset. The Catalan monarch Pedro III made an ascent of Canigou in the Pyrenees, and the poet Francesco Petrarca climbed Mont Ventoux, near Avignon, in 1336 – the first recorded climb made solely for pleasure. In 1358 Bonifacio di Rotario ascended Roccia Melone (11,600ft, 3,536m); in 1492 Domp Julien led a group up Mont Aiguille, the first recorded artificial climb in which ladders, pulleys and ropes were used; and in 1739 a Swiss monk climbed Titlis. The Englishmen Pocock and Windham brought mountaineering into the realm of sport in 1741 by their exciting adventures on the glaciers of Chamonix. Colonel Beaufoy reached the summit of Mont Blanc in 1787. Most of the expeditions had at least a veneer of scientific investigation, but when Wills climbed the Wetterhorn in 1854 there was no pretence at all – it was just for fun.

The first book on the subject was J. D. Forbes' *Travels through the Alps of Savoy* (1843), which was followed in 1859 by John Ball's *Peaks, Passes and Glaciers*. The English Alpine Club was founded 1857 with John Ball as its first president, and the French Alpine Club established in 1874.

Edward Whymper (1840–1911) was not only a mountaineer but an artist and author of considerable merit whose prose and sketches made his works extremely popular. His ascent of the Pointe des Ecrins (1864) proved his exceptional climbing ability, but his seventh ascent of the

The road to adventure

8

Matterhorn (1865) was a Pyrrhic victory, in that although the party gained the summit, four out of the seven climbers were killed when a rope snapped. Controversy ensued in which Whymper was accused (falsely, I feel) of having cut the rope to save the lives of the other three, including himself. Whymper later pioneered climbs in the Andes, Canada, Greenland, etc, and bequeathed his collection of Alpine plants to London museums. His *Scrambles among the Alps* and *Great Andes of the Equator* still make fascinating reading a century after his death.

By 1870 nearly all the highest Alpine peaks had been climbed by courageous men: Mummery had conquered the Grepon, Dent mastered the Dru – they may be said to have initiated rock climbing on the difficult pitches those two mountains present. Mummery lost his life on Nanga Parbat in 1895, shortly after the publication of his book *My Climbs in the Alps and Caucasus*.

The following five decades showed an ever-increasing explosion of mountaineering throughout the world. English climbers showed a frantic determination to achieve *firsts*: Freshfield in the Caucasus, Whymper on Chimborazo, Fitzgerald on Aconcagua, Conway on Illimani and in Tierra del Fuego, Green in New Zealand. Bruce and Norton made the first organised expedition to Everest (1922); the poet and philosopher of mountaineering, Frank Smythe, established himself on Kanchenjunga and Mt Kamet (24,431ft, 7,450m) in 1931; and Freddy Spencer Chapman, an outstanding figure in the world of mountaineering, also did a great deal of exploration in the Himalayas.

It is a fallacy to assume that good climbing can only be found in far-off places. There is difficult and exciting climbing to be found in Britain, America, Australia and South Africa, without the need or expense of furnishing expensive expeditions to Switzerland, the Himalayas, or the Andes. A large number of Swiss mountains are famed rather for the superb photography of professional photographers rather than for their real value in climbing. If you can only get to the nearest outcrop of rocks, a few hundred feet high, have no regrets, for you are probably missing nothing more than the exorbitant bills of Swiss hoteliers. Rock climbing revealed exciting routes up a mountain that before H. C. Jones' ascent of the East Peak of Lliwedd by the Paradise route (1909) were impossible.

Rock climbing developed new and athletic moves in the use of knees, shoulders, back muscles etc to deal with chimneys and crevasses, and showed that a man could balance on a mere inch or two of rock by his feet while his hands explored a still more precarious hold. Such techniques meant that hitherto inaccessible rockfaces could now be climbed. Some of the most difficult rocks in Britain were first conquered by Colin Kirkus, and these may be compared with the worst that the Himalayas have to offer – a short rock face a hundred feet high may test your technique more excitingly than some tourist-covered Swiss slope, where patience and endurance are more at stake than technique. We shall try to analyse the difference between patient endurance and pure technique. But there is, of course, another essential factor in climbing – the sheer courageous determination to go on and reach the top, as shown by New Zealander Sir Edmund Hilary and Nepal's Sherpa Tensing when they reached the summit of Everest in 1953, a unique and historical 'first'.

SIDE BENEFITS OF CLIMBING

One of the most popular attractions of this sport is the opportunity it offers to revel in beautiful scenery, which can only be enjoyed from the heights. Gazing down, one sees toy farms and fields spread out in the sunshine, and splattered with colours like a painting. Even winter climbing has its scenic compensations. A break in the clouds, for instance, may throw up a spectrum of splintered light on shining wet rock in a rainbowed rift hundreds of feet below. Little wonder that there are 295 references to mountains and 118 more to hills in the Bible – so long have they evoked men's admiration and affection.

Apart from more recent classics, such as *The Glass Mountain, The Sound of Music*, etc, some of the greatest and most beautiful films about mountains were made by Leni Riefenstahl, including the exceptionally beautiful *Das Blaue Licht*, and *Die Weisse Hölle von Piz Palü*. For the latter film the famous air ace Ernst Udet was employed to take aerial shots of superb scenery among some of the most treacherous air currents in the world.

If you are a birdwatcher, you will find many species in mountainous terrain, not least the eagles, which show a spirit of freedom and superiority wonderful to watch, largely ignoring human beings. Both the botanist and geologist also have good reason to climb, for the new knowledge they can acquire in the high country is a continual source of surprise and delight. You need not be a tiger of the rockface to find the starlike edelweiss or clumps of pretty saxifrage, and the attractions for the geologist are obvious. The photographer with colour film will want to camp in the mountains, and to take several rolls of film with him. The sun sinking into a wine-coloured sea or setting behind jagged ridges may easily give him the photograph of a lifetime.

Another attraction of mountaineering is the people you meet. Climbing creates an instant fraternity, a wealth of good companionship. Dangers met, shared and overcome together form a powerful bond that does not fade with time. In each of us danger and unusual circumstances evoke courage, determination and initiative. Every difficulty mastered is a victory milestone in our lives. The difficulties are there to be overcome, just as the resistances a weightlifter uses in a gymnasium are there to strengthen his muscles and build him up.

Self-reliance, loyalty to friends and a strong sense of duty are qualities without which you cannot survive on mountains. Man's own transience becomes apparent when you are clinging to a rockface a few thousand feet above a sheer drop into the sea of clouds that masks the land still further below – one is then little more than Lin Yu Tang's *Leaf in a Storm*.

Probably nothing develops self-reliance and presence of mind so quickly as climbing alone. The Vikings believed that the gods acquired perpetual youth by eating the magic apples of Idhunn, but breathing pure mountain air is probably a good substitute, and even very senior climbers look young and feel younger than non-climbers.

This book will enable you to approach the mountains with confidence and with knowledge, and will help you find the happiness, excitement, sense of achievement and success that climbing offers. Frank Smythe says in *The Spirit of the Hills*: 'It was getting to the summit that counted, the kingdom, not the crown.' Such an experience-filled thought helps us see all life with more hope, joy and knowledge. May you too find it ever so.

2 Before You Begin

Some Definitions

We cannot make any sense out of life unless our words mean the same thing to other people as they mean to us, so we shall start this book by defining the terms used in it.

HILLWALKING

Anybody and everybody is naturally a hillwalker, whatever their age. My father made me fight my way, unaided, up an 800ft hill, St Boniface Down, on the Isle of Wight when I was three years old! His reason for doing this was that he had done it when he was three. He was very proud of me when I achieved it then, and I am very proud of him now for urging me on. The oldest person I know who is still hillwalking fairly regularly is a Welsh lady, 78 years old, and she is very good at it.

Hillwalking is mostly done with the feet alone, though a walking stick may be carried. An occasional handhold is to be expected to ensure good balance. I class a hillwalk as any incline up to 44°.

SCRAMBLING

This starts with 45° and can get steeper. Some handholds may be needed for 25 per cent or more of the ascent. It offers more excitement than hillwalking, but not necessarily better views.

CLIMBING

Handholds are needed for about 50 per cent of the ascent. Helmets should be worn if the ascent is very steep.

DEFINITIONS

HILLWALKING - UP TO 44° INCLINE FEET ALONE ARE USED, ONLY RARELY IS A HAND HOLD REQUIRED

SCRAMBLING - 45° INCLINE AND ABOVE. SOME HAND HOLDS NEEDED 25% OR MORE OF THE ASCENT

CLIMBING - HAND HOLDS NEEDED 50% OR MORE OF THE ASCENT

ROCK CLIMBING - ROPES AND OTHER ARTIFICIAL AIDS NEEDED. ALL MOVES USING HANDS AND FEET

14

Rock Climbing

This is often an ascent of more or less vertical cliffs, and ropes, pitons, etriers and various artificial aids are needed. Virtually all moves necessitate the use of hands as well as feet.

Mountaineering

What is a mountain? In Britain it is any eminence of 2,000ft (610m) and above, and on the Continent it is generally anything of 600m and above. Mind you, in Denmark they have one called Heaven's Mountain that is barely 900ft (274m), but as it is the only one they have, we cannot complain about it. Generally a mountain is what is called a mountain locally.

Great climbers who concentrate on rock climbing never denigrate the other forms of climbing. Some pianists never get beyond playing Strauss waltzes, but their expertise shames those who play Liszt or Beethoven badly. Do what you can do well!

Height is largely irrelevant. If you can keep your head and proceed from one scant foothold to another 100ft above sea level, you should find it no more difficult physically 8,000ft higher up, though at that height, if one gazes round, it is more difficult to accept one's position. In fact it may be in many ways less dangerous at 8,100ft than 100ft. For example, any range will most likely offer you short climbs of Very Severe standard, and several outcrops of rock in what could not properly be called mountain terrain at all offer some of the most difficult climbing discovered yet. There is the Old Man of Hoy, a mere 450ft (137m), but climbing it is no child's play. Below is the ocean that sweeps the Orkneys from the untamed Atlantic, the rock comprises wholly vertical forbidding sandstone with some overhangs, and the wind blows unceasingly!

You may ascend the over-advertised Swiss Alps often without a single care, but then be caught in Wales on a mountain called Carnedd Dafydd, a mere 3,427ft (1,044m) whose sinister reputation comes from a rounded summit *wholly without distinguishing marks*. There is a sudden drop of over 1,500ft (450m) down a craggy precipice, Ysgolion duon, which falls away with no visible sign until you are on the edge. One quick sweep of cloud covering the summit and, even with a compass, a great deal of care (and courage) is needed to come down safely. I was caught with a Japanese climber on a mountain one wintry day when I thought he was carrying the compass and he was sure I was! We did have a map, but that was useless, and we were forced to grope for any cairn, any mark, that might help us find our way off Glyder Fawr. We are alone, for nobody else seemed to be out that day. He insisted that, as the more experienced climber, he should take charge, much against my better judgement I agreed (it was my first climb on the Glyders), and we ended up descending the Esgair Felen, somehow reaching the valley alive (we had no ropes – only our cameras, some lemons and glucose tablets). Then the mist cleared, and we were both sick to see what we had done when barely able to see more than a few yards ahead at any time of the 3,000ft (914m) descent. We need not have risked our lives if we had checked for the compass before starting out.

If you are a hillwalker or a scrambler do not let other types of mountaineer impose upon you; a descent made from 1,500ft (450m) on a wet chilly day, with the light fading and mist looming around, may be more difficult and dangerous than one from 10,000ft (3,050m) in June sunshine, with yodelling itinerant herdsmen and Technicolor views in the crisp dry air. Another interesting point is that not always the highest or most difficult mountains have the best views. Moel Siabod, at 2,860ft (871m) is much neglected for the Snowdon range opposite, but its beautiful views are unsurpassed, a point George Borrow made over 100 years ago.

Mountain Manners

The first rule is that members of a party remain within hearing distance of one another. There is no greater error than a leader trying to force people to keep up with his pace, though it is extremely foolish for a group to quarrel with the leader and not try to keep up with him.

Members of a party are responsible for each other's safety. Make sure you do not have a malingerer or whiner in your party *before* you set off. If you do get landed with one, you will have to take care of the extra load; possibly by the end of the trip he or she will be cured.

Plan your route before making an ascent, not while you climb, and always ensure that you know an easy route for emergency descent. All parties of the group must know where the Mountain Rescue Post/ Police are to be found.

If you meet a lone climber on the mountains during bad weather, you should ask him if he wishes to join you, especially if it is misty or snow is likely.

If there is the slightest sign of exposure, you must stop and check for symptoms. A stop in time may prevent a disaster.

If there is an accident, you must follow the correct procedure, even if the victim is *not* one of your party. To leave an injured man on the mountains without help may mean his death, and you would never forgive yourself if that happened.

Do not boast about the mountains you have climbed, especially not to less experienced climbers. You may assume their physical capability is as robust as your own, and do them and yourself injustice. Some people learn to climb in spite of handicaps and disabilities! I have known crippled people climb, and even the blind have found it exciting. If you notice somebody scrambling when you are on a rockface yourself, try to remember that ability, effort and enjoyment are relevant to physical potential as much as the courage and experience of the individual.

On Your Way to the Mountains

Never leave farm gates open if they were shut before you came to them. The sheep or cattle shut in that field may represent the farmer's entire stock.

If you climb over a stone wall, replace any stones you may knock off it.

Do not walk over a farmer's crops or vegetable plots to reach your mountain. Some people in this world are starving, and that is food growing there. Take care of it. If the way to the mountain passes over private property, go and ask for permission to cross it; unless there is an outbreak of foot and mouth disease locally, the farmer will almost certainly say yes, and probably tell you of any short cuts possible.

Do not damage wild life, wildflowers, birds, etc. Do not take eggs from a nest, for some species are already too rare. If you like the wildflowers you see, leave them for somebody else to admire or photograph them in colour. They will last longer then than if you pick them. If you are not sure what they are, take the book of identification to the plant and not the plant to the book.

Do not leave a trail of litter behind you. Do not start fires by dropping cigarettes among heather, etc.

GENERAL BEHAVIOUR

Go together, stick together, return together.

Keep one eye on the weather all the time.

Do not throw or kick stones on a mountain, for a dangerous avalanche of stones can be started this way. If you dislodge stones by accident, cry out loud 'Below!', 'Achtung!', 'Sucre!' – depending whether you are in Britain, Germany or France.

If trouble hits your party, slow down, think, use commonsense.

Always take the safe way down, even if it is longer, because you are more tired on the return than during the ascent.

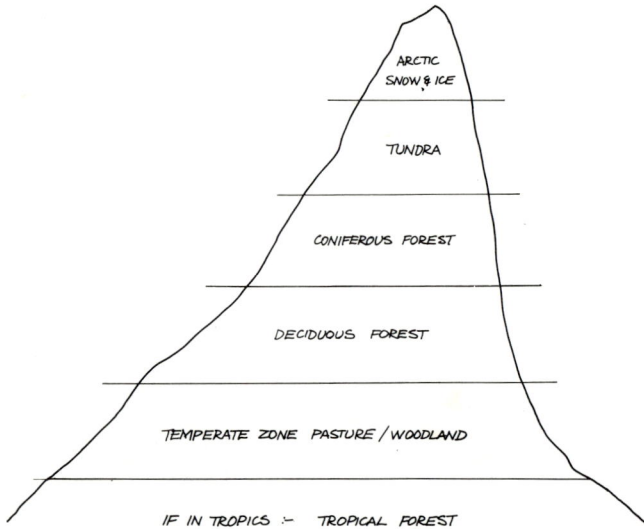

Mountain Weather

If you took a plane from Naples to Lapland, from Florida to Baffin Island, from Port Darwin to Hobart, or from Johannesburg to Bouvet Island, you would expect to find the climate considerably colder at the place of arrival than it was at the place of departure. Beginners often overlook that when they ascend a mountain they are passing through the temperate zone into the arctic.

The exact altitude at which these conditions are met with depends upon the latitude of the mountain, so that Kilimanjaro (almost on the

Equator) does not reveal arctic conditions until you reach about 16,000ft (4,877m) and Peterman Peak (Greenland) is arctic from the lowest slope upwards. The mountains found in the temperate zone often present tundra conditions at 7,000ft (2,134m) and arctic at 9,000ft (2,743m) and upwards. Climbing presents a transition from tropical forest to arctic within 4 miles (6·44km) upwards, equivalent to about crossing 45° of latitude.

This is one reason why mountains have a correspondingly high rainfall below the snowline, although the vegetation is limited to places where there is sufficient soil for it to take hold. Above the snowline the air is too cold to hold much moisture, so that there is relatively little or no rain (in form of snow or sleet). Below the snow-

Fingers of stone reach to a darkening sky, recalling Lear's 'storm clouds brood on the towering heights of the hills of the Chunkley Bore'

line the rainfall is caused by the damp-laden winds being forced to rise when they encounter the heights of the mountain, so that the windward slopes becomes covered with blanketing clouds from which moisture drips – maybe a mere mizzle, perhaps a cloudburst. To the leeward side the air drops down and warms, and rain may cease altogether; this part is known as the rain-shadow. It is a useful tip to move smartly round to the leeward side of a mountain if you are caught in a storm, provided it does not make you lose your whereabouts or stray too far from your route.

The atmospheric pressure is noticeably reduced above 8,000ft (2,440m), and people used to dwelling on the plains or at the seaside may feel, more than others, a shortness of breath. This soon reduces the energy available, and the effort of movement is noticeably more.

Pressure is measured in millibars, one of which is equal to 1·02 grams weight per square centimetre. At sea level the pressure is roughly 1,000 millibars. At 18,000ft (5,486m) the pressure drops to c 500mb, and at the top of Everest the pressure would be a mere 18mb.

Going from sea level to the peak of a 5,000ft (1,524m) mountain can mean a drop of at least 16°F (9°C) on the best of days. Winds are less restricted at great heights; on Mt Washington (6,268ft ,1,910m) speeds of over 230 miles (370km) per hour have been recorded. A low temperature always strikes damper and colder during high winds; this is known as wind chill. Winds of 32 miles (51·5km) per hour and upwards are classified as gales on the Beaufort Scale. The reason for increased windspeed is the loss of retarding friction found at ground level. An intelligent appraisal of weather conditions is required at all stages of any ascent of mountains, because weather changes more rapidly on the heights than at ground level.

Normally the lapse rate (drop of temperature) is about 5°F per 1,000ft ascended. This varies slightly with humidity, but a more severe drop is indicative of impending changes.

In the event of mist forming, take compass readings immediately just to make sure you know exactly where you are by the time the mist gets worse. When it is foggy, make sure you do not become separated from your companions.

Electrical storms occur on mountains, the electrical charges being commonly attracted to peaks, ridges, and high exposed places. Make for lower ground, where it will be safer. Frank Smythe reported seeing St Elmo's fire on the rock towers of the Pétéret ridge, on Mont Blanc;

this form of display is a silent electrical discharge between the atmosphere and rocks, trees, high masts, etc. It is recognisable by a pale blue light like a wide candle flame, but apart from its frightening appearance it is virtually harmless.

In the event of electrical storms it is often safest to discard your ice axe, crampons and obvious metal equipment and sit at some distance from it, preferably on dry rock. If that is not available, sit on rope or anything that can help insulate you from the surface. Do not sit near peaks, spires or towers of rock, or in caves or crevices, and keep away from trees on the lower slopes. The approach of an electric storm is usually heralded by an eerie buzz from ice axe, rock ridges, or any metal equipment. Sometimes your hair may start crinkling, and stand on end! Take precautions immediately!

If it begins to snow, you should seriously think about turning back. Snow in the mountains rarely drifts off; it usually comes, settles and then keeps on coming.

3 What to Wear and Carry

Clothing

Clothing has several functions. First, it excludes the wind, which, as any mountaineer will tell you, is the most exhausting and tireless foe you meet on the heights, and a principal cause of coldness. Second, it keeps out the rain, another source of cold, and a psychological deterrent in itself; if you are several thousand feet up, soaked to the skin, and near freezing as your body loses heat trying to dry off the wet cold, you cannot concentrate properly on the techniques to bring yourself safely back to ground level. Third, clothing is also required to trap air, which is in itself a good insulator, helping us to keep warm.

Clothing must essentially be lightweight, with the exception of breeches (see p 25), and tough enough to withstand the rigours of mountaineering. It should be largely made in mountain safety colours – brightly coloured orange, yellow, red or blue (vivid) – which stand out best against dull rocks when a friend or rescuer is scanning the area with binoculars to find you.

There is no substitute for wool. Normally I wear a string vest covered with a chunky Scandinavian pullover of oiled wool. Wool permits the skin beneath it to breathe comfortably and keep warm, and in hotter moments to perspire without suffocating the cells. Herodotus tells us that the Ancient Babylonians were clad in woollen tunics. The Ancient Greeks commonly wore woollen clothes, and in Roman Britain a woollen mill for making such clothing was established at Winchester nearly 2,000 years ago. Within certain limits wool, especially oiled wool, will keep you warm during a light shower of rain, but clearly you should not let woollen garments get thoroughly soaked, or they become heavy and uncomfortable. Thick Norwegian or Scottish sweaters are a boon to the climber; Swiss, Austrian and other wares are very pretty to look at, but often so thin as to be useless. Oldtimers favoured wearing two or three sweaters, but this hampers the breathing. One thick layer of wool permits the skin pores to absorb air; several layers hinder the process. A good woollen scarf or old-fashioned muffler is valuable if you are caught in a storm in winter; it can be tucked around the neck to keep out the rain and cold, and often saves wearing a second sweater (see also mitts, p 28).

I cannot recommend the down-filled jackets so popular in the Alps; they are so often badly ventilated, like many Swiss wares vastly over-priced, and nowhere near so good as solidly made British products. Such jackets are useful only for extremely high altitudes, which only advanced mountaineers reach a few times during their lives.

ANORAKS AND CAGOULES: WATERPROOF WEAR

The word waterproof is a relative term. On a ridge at 5,000ft (1,524m) or above in a gale force 7 or 8 almost nothing is waterproof; the strength of the wind drives the scudding rain through the finest mesh woven by man. Since you should have left the mountain at the first signs of such a storm approaching, we shall talk of conditions where the wind does not exceed 31 miles (50km) per hour, and the rain is a nuisance rather than a menace. For conditions up to force 6 (Beaufort scale) many garments will provide the protection you may need.

The anorak was developed from the excellent Eskimo invention of the same name. It is made of artificial fibres, and is usually a good wind-resistant garment. The long sleeves are generally extended below the wrist, or end with a close-fitting extension that would be covered by the rim of mitts, gloves, etc. It should have a permanently attached hood to be a true anorak; this hood gives protection to the base of the neck, below which all nerve centres run, and where, if you get badly chilled, numbness may seize the body. The hood may usually be closed in front by buttons or drawstring, reducing the area of face exposed to the elements. These may seem unimportant refinements when you sit at ground level and read about them, but a few thousand feet up the preservation of every possible degree of warmth is essential.

Zipped pockets in anoraks are usually covered with an extra layer of cloth to keep out rain and help prevent frosting over. There is in-variably a large map and compass pocket across the chest. For higher

ANORAK REACHES TO
TOP OF THIGHS

CAGOULE REACHES
TO THE KNEES

altitudes avoid an anorak that has a zip or buttons down the front, for the cold may creep in there. There may be punched holes under the shoulderblades to allow for breathing of the armpits, preventing condensation inside. There should be a drawstring slightly below the waist. Anoraks specially made for mountaineering usually have extra strength at the elbows and across the shoulderblades at the back. Some models have buttoned or elasticated inner sleeves to prevent the arms getting chilled.

The cagoule is an anorak extending to knee level. It completely covers the thighs but does not obscure or hinder the leg or foot movements.

Both these garments can be sprayed with liquid silicon aerosol sprays to render them more rain-resistant. Some hillwalkers wear waterproof trousers, but I do not like these much (see legs, p 26). Never have a garment so wide that it flows and flutters in the wind. Do not wear wind and/or waterproof garments unless absolutely necessary, otherwise you will perspire too much. Plastic raincoats tear too easily to be of use in mountain terrain, and cycling capes billow out too easily.

Always make sure your outer clothing is dry before putting it away. Do not even hillwalk in fancy dress. I once found two students scrambling up a slope in Moorish arbaiyas and kufeia, and wearing Ageyl headring! To cap it all, they wore plimsolls! Of such whims are fatal accidents made.

BREECHES

There are several dangers in mountaineering with bare legs, so shorts and mini-skirts are unsuitable. Jeans may be passable for hill-walking, but even then I advise against them, excellent as they are for other occasions, because they get wet and do not dry out fast enough. Breeches are best. These come slightly below the knee, and fasten up round woollen stockings. They are comfortable, allow easy movement, and, what is most important, they allow the mountaineer to see his feet where a loose piece of ledge might be concealed by trousers (particularly bell-bottoms or flares). If you are sidling along from one narrow hold to another, you must be able to see your feet and where they go. A hillwalker or scrambler on an easy scramble can (and should) roll up trousers to the knee if worn, but I strongly prefer breeches. The best material is indubitably British worsted, because it can absorb rain and still keep warm. Other materials get cold if they are wet. The breeches should have a double seat for greater insulation against cold and damp when you sit down. Molecord or whipcord are better than denim, but not so good as worsted for scrambling, climbing or rock climbing.

When the sun burns down on bare rock, the temperature can become really hot; it is possible then to loosen breeches at the knees and roll down the stockings over the rim of the boot to cool the legs. Whether you wear braces or a belt with the breeches is purely a matter of taste, but no fastening should be so tight as to cause discomfort.

Never slide down a slope of scree on the seat of your breeches, for you would be out of control and could hurtle over some precipice with no means of stopping yourself. In addition, your friends might find the ravages of the mountains on your garments a source of merriment.

I advise against the use of zip fasteners, for they can freeze up, tear cloth or jam; so use buttons, which are easy to replace and cannot freeze or jam. Pockets should have a fastening to ensure that maps, compasses, etc are not jolted out, although it is more usual to carry these in anorak pockets or rucksack. Rock climbers usually have a special long pocket in their breeches to hold a piton hammer.

Ladies are advised to wear ladies' breeches. Skirts are all right for a hillwalk or easy scramble, but unsuitable for any other form of mountaineering.

Some climbers and other grades carry light nylon over-trousers to keep in warmth, and exclude wetness and wind in bad weather. There are times, however, when it is dangerous or not possible to wear overs.

UNDERWEAR

The Muslims popularised underwear, in light cotton, over 800 years ago. Underwear has a twofold function – for cleanliness, in that it prevents sweat and soil from damaging costly outer garments; and for the insulation of body temperature against extremes of heat and cold. During World War II Norwegian string net underwear proved the best for practical purposes during hard physical exercise.

If you know you are going into very cold conditions, such as a winter climb or a hillwalk/scramble on snow or ice, it may be advisable to consider woollen underwear (Long Johns), but this is for high altitudes, and it is possible to get vests of string netwear with long sleeves. String vests come with T-shape necks or with thin straps for the shoulder (sometimes called X shapes). I generally prefer the T shape.

For all forms of mountaineering, nylon, man-made fibres, and cotton underwear are totally unsuited. They do not soak up the body's natural perspiration, and when one sweats, the wetness chills rapidly in the mountain air and remains as a cold discomfort that could induce exposure if the climber becomes tired.

SOCKS AND STOCKINGS

The older mountaineers used to recommend the wearing of two pair of socks, or stockings and a pair of socks, but in my view this is seldom necessary. I was taught to wear only one pair of good oiled-wool stockings, using additional socks only in extremely cold conditions. One pair allows you more sensitivity of foot in rock climbing.

If it is a boiling hot day, and you find you are getting unduly tired with two pairs of socks on, you should remove one pair to allow the feet to breathe more easily. Every pore on the skin's surface breathes, and you will certainly climb better if you allow them to do so.

It is sometimes said that blisters and other discomforts of the feet originate in not wearing two pair of socks, but it is more usually the fault of badly fitting boots. Feet swell when used for five or six hours

Mountain walker well-dressed and equipped for his travels

with little rest, so that you should wear a boot a size larger than your normal fitting to allow for such natural swelling, and for wearing second pair of socks if need be. In any case, always carry a second pair of socks or stockings with you to change into. If you make a cold early start in the morning (I have often started at 4.30am), it is advisable to wear socks as well as stockings. The general practice is to wear the stockings up to the knees, and the socks rolled down over the rim of the boots to prevent tickly heather, grit and small stones getting into them. With one pair of stockings only it is advisable to wear ankle-protectors, small gaiters that perform the same anti-irritant functions. These gaiters are usually made of nylon. Full calf-size gaiters can be worn in snow to add to the warmth of the leg, and keep snow and cold out of the boots.

If you wear only one pair of stockings, you should use a small piece of foam-rubber padding at the toe, to prevent stubbing when you climb or descend a steep path. The feet can be forced into angles that cause painful jarring against the hardened toe-cap of the boots without padding. Never oil the toe-cap; keep it hard, it is for your protection.

Socks must allow for elasticity of movement and circulation of air. They must also be resilient enough to lessen shocks from movement of feet over rough terrain. For this reason it is unwise to wear socks that have been darned, for the bunching together of the wool often makes an uncomfortable lump, which can raise a blister.

Avoid dyed socks. If you get a blister that bursts, or any abrasion of the skin, sweat may melt the dye, and you could get blood poisoning overnight. I have seen it happen to a friend of mine. I opt for Norwegian *ragg* or Harris wool stockings (or socks), and advise against cotton and nylon mixtures; but wool and nylon are popular in heavy snow because it is hard for snow or ice to adhere to the nylon. Cotton and nylon crinkle up easily and induce heavy sweating.

The main reason for wearing one pair of stockings for most forms of climbing, and only those who have already climbed will understand this fully, is that one layer of wool allows the toes and feet to develop an almost sixth sense of awareness, feeling the rocks below the sole more precisely for security.

Mitts

Except in special circumstances (see below), do not wear gloves of leather, for it gets wet and stays wet and cold. Wool and combinations of wool are best. Scramblers, climbers and rock climbers need fingerless gloves known as mitts. British Millarmitts are increasingly popular with mountaineers throughout the world, giving warmth, and great strength in handling rocks. Hillwalkers can wear woollen gloves or mitts.

All mitts used in any form of mountaineering must keep the wrist warm. In winter or snowline mountaineering the wrist and forearm are very vulnerable to cold; experienced oldtimers keep worn stockings, cut off the worn out foot, make a good edge to the cut part, and use them to cover from wrist to forearm. As the old Scots proverb says 'If you keep a thing seven years you'll find a use for it.'

If you are rock climbing, you need ropes, and overgloves of leather to wear on top of thin woollen ones. Leather withstands the burns of a fast moving rope better than other materials.

Hats

Hillwalkers can wear what they like on their heads as long as they have a plastic rainproof cap tucked in the pocket or rucksack. Scramblers can usually wear what takes their fancy, but if they know they are going into tough terrain, a helmet is advisable. Climbers and rock climbers are advised to wear British Standards approved climbing helmets, which are stronger in ratio to weight than other types of helmet, and can withstand falling rocks, among other perils.

Many climbers wear no headgear at all or just woollen caps – sometimes Balaclava helmets covering head, ears, neck, etc. Basically the answer is to know into what sort of terrain you are going, and what your requirements will be.

Boots

For hillwalking, scrambling and climbing you need boots; for rock climbing you need usually more specialised footwear, but you will also require boots if you have to do some ordinary climbing to reach the desired rockface. *The following information is specifically devoted to the first three classes of mountaineering.* Footwear for rock climbing is dealt with under that heading (p 59).

Whatever else you may feel tempted to economise on, do not skimp yourself when getting a pair of boots. Bad footwear is a major source of mountaineering accidents.

There are three reasons why you should wear boots while mountaineering. First, boots will protect your ankles from bruises, cuts and strains better than shoes will. A sprained ankle may be so painful that you cannot move either up or down, nor get help, warmth and shelter. It can mean being stranded for a whole night (especially if you are alone). If you are high up, the drop in temperature during the night will be much greater than that in the valley below, and this alone could make you ill. So do not neglect the dangers of a sprained ankle. Slippery rocks, movable boulders, a treacherous patch of scree, a slip on wet grass (it seems more like glass sometimes) are all traps that can ensnare the advanced climber, let alone the beginner. Minimise the danger by wearing boots!

Second, because boots stretch up to the ankle, they keep out water and mud when you traverse wet ground, leap across streams and land a bit short, or step on the edge of a bog. When feet get wet, they lose heat more rapidly, and with cold feet the whole of your body tends to cool rapidly. If your entire system becomes chilled, you will risk exposure, which can lead to death.

Third, boots last much better in rough terrain than shoes. Rocks are no respecters of persons or clothing, and least of all of footwear. Scratches, cuts, strains on stitching caused by unusual angles of pressure can rip the heart out of a nice pair of shoes in one single day's scramble.

Safety demands proper climbing boots, as the trade calls them. Before you try on the boots, don an extra pair of socks, so that you are wearing two pairs, as you might need to do when going up some wintry slope. As a rough guide, most of us take boots one size larger than the shoes we normally wear. Always try both boots on, never just one boot. When you have put them on, lace them up fully as you would for an ascent, and then walk up and down stairs two or three times, balancing just on the toe of the boot, not the entire sole. If the sole bends at all under this strain, it is of no use to you; it might bend when you are balancing on a 2in ledge 1,000ft above a sheer drop.

You may find that the pair of boots you like best, and of the right quality, cost more than you can afford. Buy them nevertheless! Go without a few meals, borrow the money, play the guitar down in the marketplace, but, whatever the cost, get the boots that feel right for you. As long as boots pinch you nowhere but in your pocket, you will be fairly safe. The fact that you put two pair of socks on to buy them does not imply that you always wear two pairs when climbing. After five or six hours on a mountain, straining against uneven surfaces, often carrying a heavier load than you endure in everyday life, the body helps the feet by increasing their blood supply; consequently they swell up, though they will return to normal size after only a short rest. Remember there must be freedom around the toes, the entire boot being broad, with no hint of tightness anywhere.

The soles of mountaineering boots should be solid, 15mm-thick, and virtually inflexible, with a broad strong heel. If you are sticking to hillwalking only you can use hillwalkers' boots (fell boots), with deeply moulded rubber soles that are slightly flexible. Some scrambling can be done in these by experienced scramblers, otherwise it is safer to keep to inflexible soles. Fell boots are cheaper than climbing boots.

Generally avoid rigid upper leather, especially round the Achilles tendon. Never tie the laces tightly.

For boots to be really waterproof, the tongues should extend right up to the rim at the top of the boots, and be sewn to the leather at every point, with gussets at the side of the tongue to make the boots easier to put on or take off. In the trade such a tongue is called a bellows tongue.

British boots usually have nylon stitching. Cheap Continental boots may seem a bargain but often lack nylon stitching, which means that the wet from mountain paths could rot their cotton stitches in a few weeks. The less stitching visible from the outside of the boot the better. There is less to be affected by stream water and sharp-edged stones.

Generally speaking, I dislike the trend towards foam rubber as padding inside the uppers of boots, for, if you fall into a stream or are caught out in a cloudburst, the foam-rubber padding takes longer to dry out than the boot, which may become rotted from within. Much more care and time is also needed to dry the boots out. Wet boots can be dried out with heated silica crystals in bags. One of them is placed in each boot overnight, and the crystals absorb the moisture.

Laces should be made of nylon, and carry two spare pairs when you climb. Eschew crosscross lacing (XXXXX) in favour of square-box lacing, which gives better support to your ankles. Tight lacing is to be avoided at all times, for it tires the feet by limiting the circulation of the blood. Lacing should extend from the rim almost down to the toes; that makes it easier to remove the boots if your feet are frozen or injured, and easier to put them on when you have changed socks because your feet are frozen or sodden through and have swollen. (Did you remember to pack that spare pair of socks?) Furthermore the nearer to the toe-cap the lacing descends, the easier it is to adjust the boots to the individual needs and comfort of your feet. Hooks are better than holes; they reduce lacing-up time, hold well, and provide less opportunity for moisture to penetrate the leather of the uppers.

Usually boots' uppers are soft except at the toes. This section of the boot should come to a strongly protected cap that can jam without discomfort into a crack of rock or balance easily on a narrow ledge without trouble.

A bewildering choice of climbing-boot soles is available. I prefer good solid British-made boots with soles cut deeper than the indent-ations on some car tyres, such as Itishide Commandos or Vibrams. Generally rubber soles are safe in all dry conditions and in snow, and fairly safe in wet weather. Rubber soles last longer than most others, but are tricky on wet grass slopes, mossed rocks and steep edges, dangerous on greasy surfaces, and poor on ice. Rubber provides a fair insulation against the cold. When the indentations flatten out, you do not have to buy new boots, just new soles, and get them properly fitted at a climbing equipment shop. In winter, crampons are needed; the best sort have quick-release straps and can be fitted over rubber soles or removed in a jiffy. It is not good to have nails, tricounis, hobs, muggers, clinkers etc, fitted over rubber soles permanently, because this combination gives you the worst results, being dangerous and unsafe.

I believe that nailed leather soles slow down the climbing pace, and make the movement upwards less fluid. Ryuzo Nakamura, the Japanese climber, always insisted that movement should be continuous and fluid. Nails are more popular for scrambling and certain climbs, but if any rock tears out one of the nails, it is most likely to take part of the leather sole with it. Nails easily wear down after one or two weeks scrambling or climbing, and reach a slipperiness that is wholly undesirable at any time on the mountains. Nails should never be used on soft rock, otherwise there will not be any rock left to climb. I prefer crampons to nails (see p 105).

Care for your boots and they will care for you. After an expedition to the hills or mountains perform the following operations:

1 Remove laces, wash them in soapy water, rinse them out, hang them up to dry.
2 Wash the boots carefully, removing grit, imbedded stones, mud, etc, before they dry into the leather of the uppers. A handful of grass will remove the worst before you leave the tough terrain for your car or home base.
3 Use a twig or a scrap of wood, but never use any metal implement to clean your boots; one simple slip could cut or weaken the leather.
4 Wet boots will need drying, especially if you are going out again next day. Never put them near a fire or direct source of heat. They will dry better left 3 or 4ft back from a stove or oven in a dry atmosphere. Never leave to another (non-climber) the task of drying out your boots. Stuff boots with dry newspaper and change this every hour or so if no other method is available. I use Dunlop's Dri-Pac, which consists of simple bags filled with chemical crystals. You heat the bags and put them in the boots overnight, and this absorbs the moisture. The bags are light to carry and very efficient.
5 When the boots are dry, polish them with silicon or wax polish. Dubbin and other oils soften the leather, and should be used only once or twice a year; more frequent use could rot the stitching. Always keep such oil clear of rubber soles, for it is bad for them.
6 When storing boots for a season, look at them to ensure there is no mildew or damage, especially inside.

The Rucksack and How to Pack It

Most mountaineers find it convenient to carry a rucksack, even for a short ascent lasting a few hours only. It has been found over many

INADVISABLE FRAMELESS DESIGN

GOOD FRAMELESS DESIGN
(FOR HILLWALKING OR CLIMBING)

A FRAMED HIGH PACK FOR
CAMPING DURING HILLWALKING

CRAMPONS

ICE-AXE

PITON HAMMER

CLIMBER'S SACK - STRAP FOR
ICE AXE - WIDE TOP - NARROW
BOTTOM

33

centuries that the best way to carry anything uphill is by putting it on the back. Hence, from the two German words *Rucken* (back) and *Sack* (bag), we have rucksack. It has some weight, even when empty, and this should not generally exceed 3lb (1·5kg). On short day trips one sack may suffice for two people, and each should have sufficient self-respect to insist upon taking equal turns in shouldering it, shifts of one hour each being ideal.

Types of Rucksack

There are basically two kinds, one with a metal frame and one without. Neither of these is perfect, and it is for you to decide which suits your purpose best.

The framed type usually weighs up to 3lb, so take this into consideration in total weight carried. It can be used up to 3,000ft (910m) quite easily. The frame keeps the bag off the back, reducing perspiration there, but can twist sideways easily and pull the unwary off balance. A waist strap can be used to make the frame more secure, but this is by no means foolproof. If you lose balance, a waist strap is dangerous, especially in high places, on windy ridges or crossing turbulent streams. If the frame or a corner of it snags on some jagged rock during scrambling or climbing, a fall could result.

The frameless type swings in against the back when you are moving, depending upon how heavy it is. Invariably smaller than a frame type, it discourages heavy loading, but causes slightly increased perspiration on the back. I generally opt for a frameless rucksack, unless camping on mountains.

Taking rucksacks in general, the shoulder straps should be at least 1½in wide, and shoulder pads are also advisable to lessen chafing and minimise taut pulling. Additional outside pockets are undesirable, especially if the pocket flaps are unfastened, because they can get trapped in a crack of rock and lead to loss of balance. One large pocket for map and compass suffice (when these are not not carried in the anorak front pocket). The rucksack should be of hard-wearing material, with extra reinforcement to base, and key corners in leather or plastic, if the ascent is expected to last more than a day.

Only a fool carries excess weight up a mountain. If the weight slows you down, you may be delayed and possibly benighted on the heights, and being lost in the dark 5,000ft up is no joke. The ideal weight for a frameless rucksack and contents is 18lb (8·2kg). This should include an extra pullover, plastic sheet and emergency rations – just in case a twisted ankle strands you high up – plus a camera and torch.

The maximum load I recommend for ascents of up to two days' duration with a frame rucksack is 30lb (13·6kg), but for a definite bivouac trip (camping) covering a long period in the mountains each member can take up to 40lb (18·1kg). One often reads of 'tigers' carrying 65lb (29·5kg) on their backs, but this is certainly not for beginners. If you want that much material, hire a helicopter to make a drop while you enjoy the climbing! The golden rule is to work out beforehand how much you *need* to carry up, which will be far less than you *want* to carry up.

For long climbs, particularly in winter, you need to have a proper climbing sack with straps to hold ice axe, crampons, etc. These sacks are very narrow, and have very broad shoulder straps, no external pockets, and a quick release strap, so that in a serious emergency the whole sack can be jettisoned. Remember that a climbing sack is less likely to suffer from a fall of 800ft (244m) than you are. Generally climbing sacks are made with extendable tops, so that at night or in tight spots the climber can put his feet and legs into them to keep warm.

Foam-rubber-padded straps or additional pads to be attached to the straps are advisable for long periods up the mountains with a sack. My rucksack always carries a length of insulated electrical wire and a bit of cord or string (about a yard or metre long) which can be used for emergency repairs to the sack if any damage is sustained at high altitudes.

The load should be carried high on the spine, and never allowed to drop down to the waist, where the bottom of the sack can dig into the body at a weak point. The load should be as high as possible and well balanced. The bottom of a frame should rest on the hipbone; if it is allowed to press on the spine, it will jolt, causing almost imperceptible shocks, and increasing tiredness.

Always dry out a sack after exposure to rain or snow. Putting it away damp or wet will produce destroying mildew. Mend any tears or cuts with patches of suitable material; if you neglect them, sudden jolting and jarring could cause them to split open and spill out some necessary item. Always wrap camera and film in two bags of polythene, one inside the other, as protection against damp and condensation.

WHAT TO CARRY WITH YOU

Remember that it is not what a rucksack weighs when you start carrying it that matters, but what it seems to weigh when you have carried it up 75° gradients for five hours. The following suggestions are not in order of importance, but rather in the order I remembered them:

Map, at least 1:50,000 (or 1in to the mile, English style).

Compass.

A whistle. Check that it works.

A torch. Check that the batteries are new and carry a spare bulb.

First-aid kit. This must include antiseptic cream, bandage, adhesive plaster, safety pins, etc. What else is needed depends on the expedition undertaken, e.g. rock climbers in high altitudes often require morphia kit.

Spare sweater/pullover, or at least a woollen scarf.

Mitts.

Woollen balaclava (if in high altitudes or during winter climbs).

Spare blanket/Heavy gauge polythene sheet to limit loss of heat if you are obliged to spend a night out or are trapped.

Cagoule/anorak (if not worn). Definitely lightweight.

Rope, maybe 120ft (36·6m) or 100ft (30·5m) length, usually carried outside sack, draped round the shoulders. Only take it if ascent demands it, never for show!

Food. Take barley sugar sweets or glucose sweets, nuts, sultanas, grocers' dried fruits (apples, apricots, etc), chocolate, tomatoes, lemons, and salt (a must). For emergency rations British Kendal mint cake in slabs is indispensable, and quite the best thing to eat high up. Do not carry brandy. Leave that to Swiss dogs, for it causes serious loss of body heat; I know the Swiss guides recommend it, but some of them seem to recommend alcohol regardless of medical knowledge.

Two spare pairs of bootlaces.

Camera, roll of spare film (one never has enough). If you must carry telephoto lens, etc, try to carry your own. Do not ask your companions to carry them, though if they offer, that is another story.

If camping out, you will need matches, meta stove, perhaps a lightweight aluminium screen against wind, metaldehyde fuel, etc.

Sleeping bags and other camping gear can be shared out to even up the weight for the man who is carrying the tent. If you cannot carry your share of gear without a groan, please do not go.

Always pack the sweater next to the back of the rucksack, so that it

36

cushions your spine against shock from angular items such as cameras. The lightest items are packed at the bottom, the heaviest on top, to relieve pressure on the spine; the shoulders are stronger and can bear the heavier load much more easily.

A sleeping bag, if carried, is usually put right at the bottom of the sack, and it is well to wrap it in a layer of lightweight gauge polythene against dampness and condensation. The meta stove and fuel and food should be kept handy near the top of the rucksack/climbing sack in which they are carried. First-aid kit also must be packed near the top of any sack, for it may be needed in a hurry. A small compact first-aid pack can be carried in an anorak pocket if this garment is worn.

Establish check lists of what is to be carried, especially *who* is responsible for bringing the matches, for every type of expedition made. If you go scrambling with Susan, Ted and Bill, for instance, keep a list of what you pack when with them, and another list altogether for what you carry when you do the vertical rock climbs with Harry.

Always keep your check lists near the rucksack when at home. Most human beings are depressingly the same in their habits, and most of us leave packing to the last moment, so do use these check lists. It is such a long way down just because you forgot the map or the salt.

4 Hillwalking

This is the way nearly all mountaineering begins, and unless you are reasonably successful in the techniques it demands it may not be safe for you to venture into other forms of mountain exploration and travel.

PLAN WHERE YOU ARE GOING

Choose which route you want for ascent and descent, and stick as closely as you can to it. Always leave an intelligible summary of your plans with a reliable person, and do not forget to add a line about your expected time of return. For example:

> Climbing west slope of Highview Peak.
> Descent by NE ridge and blue hills.
> Expect return 18.00 (5 Feb).
>
> *Don and John*

If you should get into any trouble, such a simple note could save lives by telling a rescue party where to search for you. If they have to waste hours looking for you, they may arrive too late.

TAKE A MAP

Use at least 1:50,000 (metric) or 1in to 1 mile (English). You must learn all the signs for contours of height (usually marked in 50ft intervals, even on metric maps), paths, cliffs, streams, bogs, pools, etc. The idea is that you can then interpret them at a single glance – for instance, if you were lost at night and only had one single match by which to read that map. Looking at the map, and referring to the interpreting signs at the bottom (or top) corner is not good enough. You must be able to *read* it. A map is a concentrated book of extremely

This almost architectural mountain range could be one of folk singer John Denver's 'rocky cathedrals that reach to the sky'

valuable information that tells you in a few signs what several pages of writing would be needed to convey. Look carefully at the contour lines on the side of a mountain; the map puts them closer together when the slope is steep, and it will show by sign if the ascent is a sheer drop, craggy or a gentle climb. The darker the shading of the incline, the higher the mountain (the signs are international). This means that by reading a map correctly you can safely make a path for yourself where none exists (according to the map).

Do not think it will be easy to follow a stream. The easiest way for water to flow is a bad path for men to follow. The sides of streams are usually filled with wet and slippery rocks. Water descends by the quickest and steepest routes, and it is sometimes near suicidal to follow some Alpine streams. When planning your route, always trace a stream to its source, because the points at which you cross it (by jumping or fording) may become few and dangerous at certain stretches of its course; huge boulders, treacherous rapids and falls may indeed make it impossible to cross.

When You Climb, Keep Height

The golden rule is to keep your height and conserve your energy. When you gain a certain height, stay there, unless it means traversing a bit of landscape that would unnecessarily consume time and energy. But always make sure you work out the quickest *safe* way down in an emergency. Generally avoid geometric planning of a route. What appears the shortest distance between two points on a map, a simple straight line, will never be so in high country. It will possibly take you across treacherous scree, a thigh-deep bog, a river in spate, or a waterfall far too wide for you to jump.

The art in planning for a hillwalk is to avoid time-consuming delay. The loss of two or three hours may mean you are stranded after dark in terrain you do not know adequately, and create purely unnecessary risks.

The Time it Takes

Do you know how fast you walk? You should check this and find out whether you are average, faster than average or slower than average. How long have you for your trip? What time will you start? At the usual speed how long will you take to walk five miles, allowing an extra hour for every 1,500ft (457m) ascended? What month of the year is it? When will dusk descend over the trails? In winter allow for an earlier start just in case rain clouds make the twilight seem sooner. Allow longer than you would think for the descent of a long hillwalk, on the grounds that you may be more tired than during the way up, when the sun was shining and an exaltation of larks enlivened the morning air with their song. As a general guide young people take one hour for each 3 miles (4·8km) walking. Older people should allow 2½ miles (4km), and both young and old should add one hour for each 1,500ft of ascent. For example:

Mount Tomcat is 3,000ft (910m) high, so the ascent means two hours up and two hours down (total four hours). The route is 6 miles up and 6 miles back, so 12 miles would take another four hours. The expedition therefore takes eight hours, plus one hour's allowance for tiredness or emergencies. Total nine hours.

Who is the Leader?

In every group of four or more there should be an accepted leader – the person with most experience and knowledge of the terrain and the techniques required to make the ascent and descent. Clearly, if none other can, the leader must be able to read a map, take a compass bearing accurately, and be able to make sensible decisions in emergency and crisis. He should also be able to recognise symptoms of exposure and know how to deal with them. On any expedition with a large group the leader should have knowledge of first-aid. If you dislike the word leader, use the word pathfinder, with its delightful overtones of Fenimore Cooper. Leadership is not bossiness, but calmness, gentle advice-giving, courage and sufficient firmness to keep any laggards on their feet. It requires a talent for getting on with people and seeing that they get on with each other, and keeping a good rhythm in the group's progress.

The Compass

Generally mountaineers take a liquid-filled compass with them, for it is the easiest to read, and there is less wobbling of needle when held by the hand in some precarious position. Take a map, place it out on the ground (or table if practising at home), and look for the diagram showing the directions North, South, East and West. Take your compass and place it over this diagram so that the fixed spearhead on your compass that says north matches exactly the line on the map pointing north. Now turn the map and the compass on top of it until the moving needle (coloured end) also matches north, so that the arrowhead on the map, the fixed spearhead on the compass and the moving needle (coloured end) all point northwards. Then your map is correctly set to agree exactly with the entire countryside around you. Now you can begin to line up which hill is where. This helps you identify all the landmarks around you, and even if you are in a fog or cloud you will know your position. Make certain there are no knives, cameras, radios, or metal objects near the compass when you take your bearing, for they might disturb its accuracy.

Now that you know your bearings, you see that the place you have to reach lies at 60° exactly from your present position. Examine the map carefully, can you safely walk in a straight line to where you want

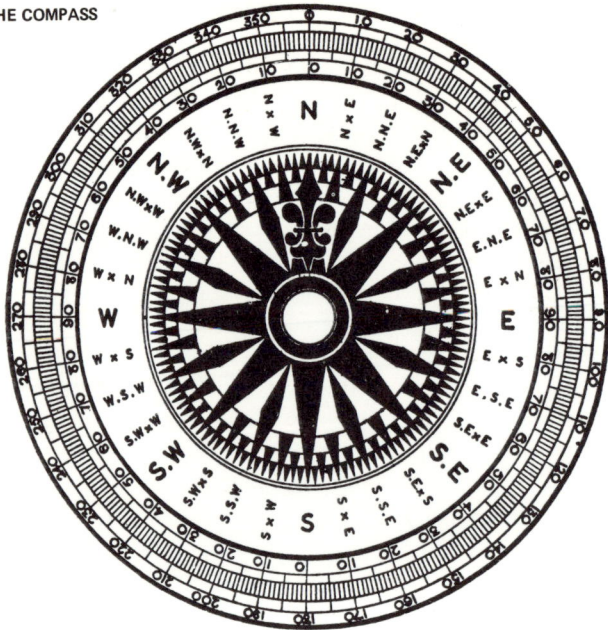

to go? Maybe the map says you must walk at 60° for 3 miles, make a detour round the edge of a precipice for 1 mile, then you can continue straight on. Measure the distances carefully. Remember that bogs, gullies, rough boulders and scree will slow down your rate of walking; it is often quicker to make a couple of miles detour over really smooth terrain than to take a seeming short cut that slows down the pace. If you find this an exciting thing to do, you could also contact one of the orienteering clubs. In the sport of orienteering there are races based upon travel with compass and a map, and the winner is the one who can estimate correctly the shortest route, including detours. My friend Petri Issakainen was distinguished for orienteering when he served in the Finnish Army (where this sport is considered essential), and covered long distances at night with only a small torch, a compass and a map, over almost virgin arctic forests and swamps. You can practise in any field or small town, and the more you practise, the easier it becomes.

FIT FOR HILLWALKING

Do not assume automatically that you are fit to walk for six or ten hours on the hills. Sitting in an office, school, or lecture room, or standing in a shop or at a factory lathe, etc, are no guarantee that your body will accept this exercise without protest. When you decide to go on the mountains, try to get some exercise beforehand. Take some practice walks regularly before you go; maybe a run round the streets in a track suit at night when you have finished work will help. Nobody would leave a car in the garage for a year and then take it out for a run without making sure it was in good condition, and a lot of people neglect their bodies worse than their cars.

Fitness is quite irrelevant to age. I have seen several septuagenarians outwalk and outclimb youngsters barely a third of their age. Remember that fitness is one of the factors that will determine whether you enjoy your mountaineering or not.

How Fast Is Too Fast?

One way to find out is simply this. Can you talk, whistle or sing while you walk the hills or scramble. This criterion does not apply to climbing or rock climbing, although on occasions I have talked while climbing difficult patches.

The Japanese climber Ryuzo Nakamura and I talked frequently about the artistic woodcuts of Hiroshige (1797–1858) and of Hokusai (1760–1849), and of the martial art of Aikido (in which he was my first instructor), and about the books of Lafcadio Hearn when we were climbing. My good Swiss friend, Kurt Müller and I wandered over the Sieben Churfürsten and Säntis in St Gallen, Switzerland, laughing about the *Novellen* of Gottfried Keller, which he had persuaded me to read. It was he who introduced me to the amusing tales of Wilhelm Hauff (1802–27) whose fairy stories I was, two decades later, to translate into English.

The mountains are a wonderful place for really deep conversations, but there are some places where silence impresses itself upon you. I was climbing with a Finnish friend, Petri Issakainen, one day in North Wales, and we stopped short in the midst of an informal chat about the poems of Viktor Rydberg (1828–95) when the clouds rolled back suddenly to reveal a sunlit panorama that took our breath away. It was some time before either of us could speak.

A useful tip is to count in hundreds if you are alone and covering a difficult pitch.

Never go so quickly that you sweat. Perspiration saps energy and robs your body of moisture under what are usually dehydrating wind conditions. Furthermore wet moisture on the body and clothing can chill quickly in wind and at high altitudes. It is a good idea to add a pullover to your clothing while you rest at high levels to avoid cooling rapidly. Aim for a steady slow rhythm, placing each foot carefully in a position you can see; if you start too fast you will tend to stop when the going gets steeper, which is a psychological set-back.

Keep a rhythmic swing to your movements, altering the length of the steps but not the rhythm. Ignore complaints that the pace is too slow from any inexperienced members of the party, for you will get to the top before they do. Starts, spurts and stops lead to disaster. Plan positive timed rests, and when you stop (maybe five minutes per hour, or ten in two hours), do not allow members of the party to wander off, play around, etc. Keep together and rest, sitting or lying on the ground with the feet up on the rucksack. Remember to insulate the body against possible damp ground.

Unless you are a goat, there is no excuse for frequent stops to nibble nourishment. Digestion absorbs energy, so that it is better to eat only when you have reached the summit. You will feel more like celebrating then.

Frank Smythe left us this good advice: 'The skilful mountaineer lounges uphill; his speed is such that he enjoys the scenery and the climbing all the time. Immediately he ceases to enjoy either he is going too fast.'

WHITHER THOU GOEST, I WILL GO

A party on a mountain might well echo the ancient words of Ruth. Beginners especially should stick to paths and tracks that are recognisable, and a party must stick together. Only fools or very bad climbers straggle; all members of the party must be in earshot of one another, close enough to hear a call. Tracks and paths are usually distinguishable by the wear and tear of other bootmarks before your own. Very often rocky patches will show signs of nailed boots having passed over them, so, if in doubt, bend down and look closely. There may be danger of exhaustion if too much is undertaken on the first ascent of a holiday

'*The silence was so heavy it could be felt*' (*Kipling*)

in the mountains. There is much more likelihood of exhaustion (physical and psychological) if a climber who has only done hillwalking is rushed straight from that into rock climbing. Do try not to miss a stage in the logical progression. The time to watch out for straggling, which may be a sign of approaching exhaustion, is during the descent – the long plod homewards.

FEET AND HOW TO USE THEM

Once you have learnt to walk in a rhythm that allows you to breathe easily and comfortably, watch how you place your feet. Correct footwork can take a lot of wasted effort and loss of energy out of climbing. Here are some hints to help the beginner:

1 Lean forward slightly. This lessens the strain on your leg and thigh muscles, and on your lungs.
2 Not even ballet dancers walk on their toes all the time. Beginners will find it easier to keep their heels loosely on the ground to minimise the stress on ankles and calf muscles. Try to place each foot down fully on its sole in a well balanced position. With a little practice it is possible to do this in rhythm.
3 When you come to a steep slope, it is easier on the muscles if you take a zigzag course up the gradient. Most well worn tracks go up in this way.
4 If you are on a wet slippery gradient, do not wear out your muscles by fighting every single slip the foot makes, but learn to let each foot slide back an inch or two. In wet weather grass is more treacherous than ice. Rock is firmer and surer in wet weather.
5 Never walk over grass near an edge of a precipice, it can let you slip and give no possible hold or delay to help you.
6 Do not lean back, but keep the weight of the body slightly forward when descending. Bend the knees also. This lessens the jarring of the foot at each step, and so reduces the shock impact to the spine, barely perceptible at the time but each shock adding up to a cumulative tiredness. Bending the knees is essential on rough terrain or uneven scree (if you are walking down it).
7 If you are experienced enough to run down scree, you must be wearing boots, and hold both legs stiff throughout, forcing your heels into the scree every time they touch ground.
8 Heather is fairly safe, since its roots are very tenacious and do not generally give way easily – except where there is a broken terrain with boulders mixed in with heather. Try to avoid such areas, because the heather will cover some nasty holes, and you may easily break an ankle.

9 Where possible, avoid grass with a covering of ice or snow. It is very treacherous.

10 Bracken commonly grows on mountain slopes, and frequently it is full of clouds of midges and other unpleasant stinging insects all anxious to have a meal at man's expense. Snakes commonly like thickets of ferns. Owing to its toughness and thick undergrowth, such vegetation will slow down your progress considerably. The roots are brittle and it is unwise to place a foothold or take a grip on bracken; in nine cases out of ten it will let you down.

11 Hillwalking and other forms of mountaineering can be almost as wet as swimming, especially if you have to traverse many bogs. Remember that on a mountain the quickest route between two points is hardly ever a straight line. You can recognise a bog by its darker shade of green, a special smell of dampness, and sometimes by the growth of whitish cotton grass in its midst. Unless you are a herbalist looking for medicinal mosses, bogs are a nuisance; they are rarely dangerous but slow down your progress, are tiring to cross, and are usually alive with insects, especially the stinging kind. Avoiding a bog saves climbing time, and the chore of cleaning up your gear when you get back to base.

Leave No Trail Behind You

Do not leave papers, chewing-gum wrappers, tobacco pouches, polythene luncheon bags, tins, plastic cups, or old banknotes behind you. Who wants to find junk like that spoiling the wilderness? If you accidently kick a large boulder out of place, try to replace it, for most rocks support plant and insect life invisible to the naked eye but useful to the ecology of the area. Never 'garden' a slope unless it is to save a life. Gardening in climbing circles means clearing all plant life off a ridge to make it easier to stand on, and leads quickly to rock erosion.

Learn When to Turn Back

Study the weather signs, and recognise when a day is going to turn out badly.

> The climber who sadly turns away,
> Will live to climb another day.
> Do you remember Loopy Strong?
> Who swore the weather forecast was wrong?
> When others turned back he went ahead,
> But they're alive, and Loopy's dead.

This applies particularly to the more advanced type of mountaineering. It is apparent to all intelligent people that the utmost discipline is required to turn back – it is not a matter of courage.

Beginners are frequently inclined to ignore weather signs. Examination of the cloud formation should help you decide whether the storm is to be of short or long duration. Listen carefully to weather forecasts before you set off. Obviously showers or light rain, while making greater care on rock and grass needful, should not be a deterrent, but a wind of force 7 – a moderate gale on the Beaufort scale, with winds of 28–33 knots or above – requires you to be extremely careful, and winds of forces 8 or 9 are good reasons for turning back; in high exposed places such winds may be inordinately powerful.

The season of the year is some indication as to whether a storm is likely to pass or settle in for the night. If it is winter and a light snowfall or sleet begins when you are 300ft (91m) from your destination, that fall may have become a blinding blizzard by the time you are in the identical position on the return journey. Use your wits!

GUIDEBOOKS

Fortunately many good mountaineers have compiled guidebooks that outline in every detail the ways in which you can ascend a mountain, and they cover many aspects from hillwalking to rock climbing. Even in the Alps, for those who cannot afford £25 a day (and tips) to some Swiss guide, there are very good guidebooks. Probably the best ever written were W. A. Poucher's *Welsh Peaks*, *Scottish Peaks*, *Lakeland Peaks*, etc, which provide a perfect pictorial guide by one of the best photographers of mountains of all time. Many of his beautifully clear scenic shots are overmarked with a thin white line showing the exact track to follow.

Guidebooks are often more accurate than guides. I recall asking an expert on one occasion how the climb we were doing was classified. 'Easy', was the reply. Later I found out from two guidebooks that both classified it as difficult, which is what I felt it to be.

DRINKING FROM MOUNTAIN STREAMS

It is usually safe to do so if the water is moving and above farmland, for farm animals have no reluctance to urinate by or in a stream from which they drink, sheep especially. If in doubt, wash the mouth out with the water and then spit it out. Always drink in moderation; if you drink heavily you will sweat more and tire, owing to the loss of mineral salts. Do not carry water up a mountain with you. It is heavy, even in plastic containers, and will do more harm usually than a few hours' thirst. In winter remember that ice melts more easily than snow, and gives you more water than snow does. It is unwise to carry with you very dry food, which would increase thirst. Salt enables the body to carry moisture better, for one grain of salt holds 70 per cent of water, but it makes you very thirsty, and should only be taken when needed. It is generally unwise to drink spirits on the mountains, because this affects the body's normal mechanism for regulating heat, causing rapid loss.

Politeness Costs Nothing

You go climbing for the experience, adventure and pleasure it is not possible to acquire in towns. Do not spoil this for other people, for your companions, especially not for the local inhabitants, most of whom have to wrest a difficult living from the terrain that provides you with so much fun. Observe the following rules:

1 Shut gates, so that sheep or livestock will not stray. Even if you fail to see the stock (it may be a day on which they are all being shorn or dipped), still shut the gates.
2 If you dislodge part of a stone wall or fence while crossing it, stop and replace the fallen part. I know of one farmer who stopped all access to a mountain he owned because of damage to his fences and consequent loss of livestock.
3 Please do not take a transistor radio with you if you intend to play it throughout the climb; others may want to listen to the birds or maybe enjoy the sheer silence of the mountains. You can indeed listen to silence. 'The silence was so heavy it could be felt', said Kipling.
4 None of us own the Earth, so if you do pick some flowers on the way back, do not strip the patch bare.

Sheep Tracks

Beware of following these upwards. Sheep seldom want to ascend to the peak of a mountain, as you do. But you certainly can follow them down, for sheep always know the safest route to comfort and security. Sheep tracks can easily be mistaken for man-made tracks, but test them for width and you will find that they are always too narrow for our comfort.

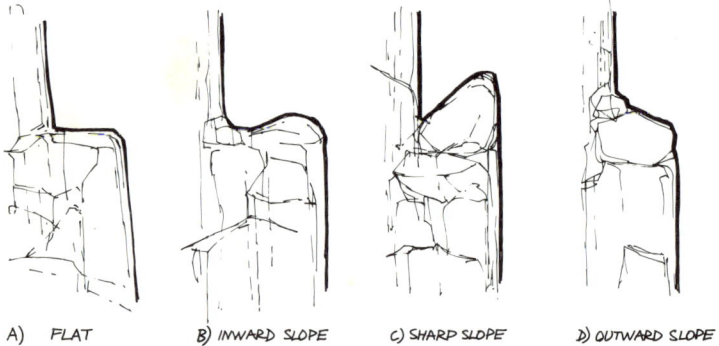

A)   FLAT   B) INWARD SLOPE   C) SHARP SLOPE   D) OUTWARD SLOPE

GENERAL HOLDS – FOR FEET

1. IN DESCENDING ORDER OF STABILITY FROM A) – D)
2. IT IS SAFER TO RISK A TRICKY STEP FROM A) OR B) BECAUSE IT IS EASIER TO BALANCE IF THE STEP HAS TO BE RETRACED SUDDENLY

GOING DOWN

No expedition on the mountains is ever over until the last member of the party has safely returned to base. The descent is often the hardest section of any trip, partly because the people are euphoric with their success in reaching their goal, partly because they are more tired (and therefore more careless) than during the ascent, and partly because there is a tendency to take short cuts. Never accept the idea that a route must be safe; some crumbly crags are just not apparent when viewed from above rather than from below. It is essential not to rush down, and to keep rest intervals during the descent as well as on the ascent.

5 Scrambling and Climbing

By my definition scrambling is done on inclines of 45° and steeper, with handholds needed for approximately 25 per cent of the ascent and climbing requires handholds for 50 per cent of the ascent. Helmets must certainly be worn for the latter, but they are optional for the former. Although scrambling and climbing are 'same pudding, different gravy', the techniques are basically the same, so that they are combined in this chapter.

In the life of every hillwalker there comes a time when he sees that a scramble over some rocks would save him perhaps half an hour's walk round a path, and if the weather is fine and dry he should take the opportunity; but in wet weather or an emergency (perhaps going to get help for a friend with a sprained ankle) he should not.

The following rules should be observed:

1 At all times three limbs should be in firm contact with the rock – either two feet and one hand, or two hands and one foot. Only one hand or one foot at a time should be moving around in search of another hold. This procedure must become second nature to you.

2 Every hold should be tugged or tapped slightly to test whether it is safe before your full weight is put upon it. This must become a habit, or a totally unnecessary accident can result.

3 Use the arms to balance yourself, and climb with your feet. There are clearly times when you pull with the arms to reach a safe hold, but if you let yourself develop into a regular puller, your arms will tire too easily.

4 Now here is the rule most neglected by scramblers, climbers and rock climbers. If it was observed faithfully, very few accidents would occur, so try to keep it well to the forefront of your thinking. Never make a move that cannot be reversed. If you move from foothold A here to foothold B over there, can you step back if you find there is crumbling rock beyond point B? Look ahead, think ahead!

5 In scrambling and climbing find support for the heels wherever possible. It looks very daring and stylish to balance on your toes, but although this is often needful, try and support the entire foot, especially the heel, because this establishes a much better balance. In all walking uphill the thrust must come from the heel, not from the toes.

6 Do not reach for high handholds when scrambling and climbing. Aim to keep the arms between the shoulders and the waist. This does not apply to rock climbing, and when you find it is natural to reach out for some higher hold without any thought of losing balance, you are ready for stiffer (probably rock) climbing. Even an advanced climber keeps this golden rule, although he often makes exceptions where experience and instinct tell him it is safe to do so.

7 Plan your route by pitches, not step by step. The dangerous climber is the fool who goes from rock to rock until he is in a jam. You must learn to check with a guide or guidebook which way to go up a mountain. You see that a walk uphill will take you to a ridge, then there is a scramble up some boulders, from somewhere further left at the top of the boulders is a tough climb leading to a ridge, and after that you only have to walk along that second ridge to the top. Planning to do a climb in pitches also gives you a chance to wait for the entire party to assemble in between pitches (and a sly rest for the leaders while others catch up with them).

8 Slow, rhythmic, smooth climbing avoids jerks, strain and tiredness. The only time you should expect to feel tired is when you sit down over a cup of tea (or coffee) down in the valley at the end of the expedition.

9 Stick to ridges and shoulders when there are no paths or tracks. These give safer, better, drier ascents, provide the better views, and permit easier visible means of retreat if a sudden change of weather makes return advisable.

10 Scree is for descent, not ascent. This is a rule that may be bent in some cases. There is a way up to the saddle of Pen y Gadair, Cadair Idris, N. Wales, by a steep scree, but it saves a lot of time and many use it. But generally only use scree for coming down.

11 Some movements on the mountains call for a traverse, which implies that one foot must move right across the other. It is safest to keep the moving leg between the rock and the standing leg.

12 Keep the body away from the rocks. This seems unnatural for the beginner, but it is essential for the body to be curved outwards away from the rock. If it is close to the rocks, you cannot see your feet nor can you see where you are putting them. If the body is curved outwards, there is more pressure of the feet inwards towards the rock.

13 Goats are allowed to jump from crag to crag, but humans must never hop

A peak like a needle scratching the sky

or jump from one foothold to another. Swing across, but always have three limbs in contact with the rocks. Occasionally a traverse from one position sideways to another requires more balance with the hands than is usual, but you cannot hope to balance on rock with a hop, skip and a jump.

14 Move! Even if backwards! Too long in one position can rob you of courage. Often you may find you have advanced with a right foot where the left foot would have been better to enable you to progress to the next hold; if you cannot do a traverse swing-through step, reverse to last position and regain this with the correct foot. If you are slow in finding footholds, or working out which foot to put where, you are showing signs of inexperience or tiredness.

15 The way to ascend a slope of steep boulders is to climb diagonally across it, which lessens the likelihood of a dislodged boulder cracking open the head of somebody below. If anything is dislodged you shout out loud 'Below!' ('Achtung!' or 'Sucre!' in German- or French-speaking lands). If you hear a shout, crouch in as close to the rocks as you can, or find the most immediate shelter, preferably below a boulder, so that if the fall approaches you, it will bounce over your head.

16 If a member of your party gets cragfast – stuck to the rocks and unable to move – get one or two above him, for a 'frozen' climber always finds it psychologically easier to go up than down. Be gentle and patient; it may be the person's first time out, or the initiation to a climb beyond anything he/she has tried before. A quick safe pull and the victim is freed. Say no more about it.

17 On small broken rock use shorter steps. Extra care is needed to test each handhold and foothold before trusting it with your weight. If the pitch is one of broken rock (smaller than boulder size), aim to keep the heels well placed, avoid toeholds where you can, and do not reach higher than shoulder height for handholds.

18 Do not hesitate on smooth slabs of slight gradient. When you find a nice smooth slab of rock with an easy angle, it is apparent that it can be climbed. It is essential to be positive and decided in your approach to such slabs. You can do it, as long as you do not hesitate, because although they usually provide perhaps a half-inch point on which to balance a boot (with stiffened sole for climbing), they are no places to stop for admiring the scenery or powdering a nose.

19 Work out with your eyes first which way you will go up the slab. You should allow that one or two holds that look feasible from below may be too thin or slippery for you when you are up there. So check from below. Is there a chance to move sideways and zigzag up?

20 Put the flat of each foot firmly on the slab. This means flexing the ankle and bending the body forwards at the waist. If at any time the feet start

slipping, straighten up out of the crouch position until the slide stops, then continue as before. The same procedure applies if you descend by such a slab.

21 Keep calm on the ridges. Well, we know one must keep calm all the time on a mountain, but a ridge is an exhilarating place to be, on top of the world. It is also a place where sudden weather changes are usually first apparent. If a swirl of wind brings a misty mizzle of rain to swathe you in seeming blindness, and you can see barely a body length in front of you, do not decide to drop over one side of the ridge in a desperate attempt to escape. Slow down, take a deep breath, get the map and compass out, ascertain whether you are nearer the goal or the starting point, and proceed according to the logic of the situation.

22 Safety does not always lie in turning back. This is a general rule as well as a special one for being cut off by weather on a ridge. If you are nearer the goal (summit) of the mountain than your starting point, there may be shelter there, where you can eat your sandwiches – maybe, if it is winter, one of you is carrying a flask of warm tea or coffee. There you can pause, rest and make further calculations to match the emergency. Perhaps, at the end of the ridge, there is a plateau with a longer but safer descent than your original choice.

23 Never reject a longer but safer route down in any emergency. Think of it this way: the route that brings you down most safely is the quickest one for any emergency. Maybe you want to get help for a friend who has fallen and is injured. If you become a casualty through taking a careless risk, you cannot help your friend or yourself.

24 Make a mental map of the track followed and of the scenery visible. In all types of scrambling and climbing it is useful to memorise by casual glances any unusually shaped rocks, or striking bits of scenery. Then if you lose the map or have an emergency you may be able to find your way back by the mental trail you have blazed.

25 Take a watch with you. By using the information given in this book about the times taken for climbing generally, you can estimate whether you are keeping to schedule, how long you should rest, etc. Furthermore it is easy to use a watch as a compass as shown in Figure 9.

26 In ice and snow leave a ridge as quickly as possible. This book is written for the beginner, and although some risk is quite justified in rain or mist, the beginner should not hesitate to get off a ridge if it starts to snow, and freezing makes moisture turn to ice. But see rule 21 above, and do not drop down from the ridge haphazardly.

27 If you find yourself in a precarious position made worse by snow – perhaps some very narrow ridge now covered with snowflakes – there are two possibilities open to you: (a) use a scarf or gloves to brush the snow away from each foothold before it is used; and (b) if you have rubber-soled boots

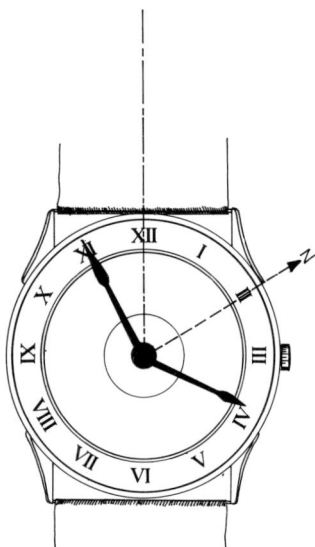

1. POINT FIGURE 12 AT THE SUN
2. HALFWAY BETWEEN 12 AND HOUR
   HAND IS DUE NORTH

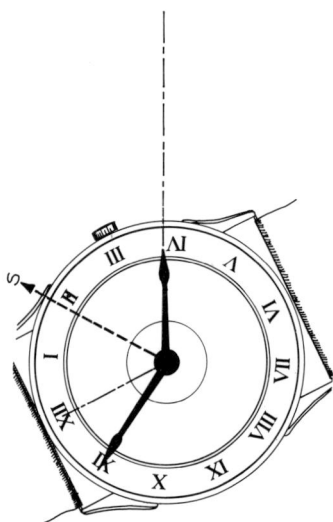

1. POINT THE HOUR HAND AT THE
   SUN
2. HALFWAY BETWEEN 12 AND HOUR
   HAND IS DUE SOUTH

(which slip more easily in such conditions), take them off and cross the dangerous area in stockinged feet. This is a last resource; the area must not be long or you can suffer from exposure as a result of the experience. If you are canny about the weather, and if you think ahead, the situation should not arise; but if it does, remember that stockinged feet are less likely to slip than rubber soles.

28 Watch the scree. Safe scree is composed of small stones more or less the same size as each other, descending in a chute or fan down a visible track. Dangerous scree is composed of stones, rocks and boulders all mixed up together. The mountaineers' dream of running down the scree is only possible on good safe scree, never on stones and rocks of mixed sizes. If in any doubt, do not run down it. It is absolutely essential to have the end of the chute or fan clearly in view before you walk down, let alone run down scree.

29 If you are descending the mountain homeward-bound, flushed with success, do not relax your vigilance. Do not descend by following watercourses. Water follows its gravitational path of least resistance, and you could need wings to pursue it. If there is no distinct known trail downwards, avoid watercourses, keep away from canyons and gullies, and beware of scree slopes.

30 When going down, think ahead. You must be able to see where a pitch leads to before you follow it; if you cannot, in mist or darkness, you have to be very good with compass and map. You can keep an eye on the descending channel of a rivulet or stream, but follow it at a parallel distance. Always look at the immediate pitch of slope to be descended, never at distant church spires, villages, farms far below. If you come across a sticky, crumbling or slippery patch of mountain, retrace your steps upwards, check the area and try for another way down that pitch.

6 Rock Climbing

It is the height of folly to attempt rock climbing without having proved to yourself that you are at home with the mountains as a hill-walker, scrambler and climber. Without this background you will not have the feel of the mountains. This fact has been expressed by poet and playwright Franz Werfel, who said: 'For those who believe, no explanation is necessary, for those who do not believe, no explanation is possible.' A good rock climber must have a sympathy for the mountain he is climbing, and to some extent this is true for the climber, scrambler and even the hillwalker.

Beginners in rock climbing should not go alone or with another beginner; an experienced rockman or instructor should be present on each ascent. Without proper tuition you are risking your life. Rock climbing is a dangerous sport, however attractive and exciting it may be. Do not try it with somebody who lacks mountain experience.

Rock climbing is not learnt high up on the mountains but by making use of a good boulder 10–12ft (3–3·5m) high. The idea is to avoid anything more than double your own height, so that if you slip while learning, the fall should be negligible. You can learn the techniques at this height without having to contend with the wind, weather and exposure of the high mountains.

'Exposure' here means the emptiness behind and below you; the greater the drop, the more windswept the place of climbing, the more exposed the ascent is said to be. An 800ft (244m) drop on an incline of 45° to the leeward of a mountain is less exposed than a 500ft (153m) vertical drop on the windward corner. It is a matter of commonsense. On some climbs the unexpected becomes a hazard, as some on sea cliffs, where climbers have reported being attacked by waves of irate seagulls. This sounds humorous to a beginner, but experienced climbers know it to be a real peril.

You must be calm, relaxed and decisive to make a good rock climber, and your psychological approach to difficulties also plays a part. A slab of rock 4,000ft (1,220m) up may be easier than that boulder you first started on a couple of years back, but this time there is a drop behind you, going a long way down. How much does that worry you? With proper precautions, climbing is no more dangerous than crossing a main road during the rush hour, but one has always to be calm and collected, and to be reasonably agile.

I once found a lady of generous proportions cragfast on an extremely simple ledge, glued there by sheer panic. I got her off and put her safely on the pathway down. What she was doing alone on a mountain, taking what she thought was a short cut, and in ordinary walking shoes, I was never able to discover. A rock climber must be able so to concentrate on the moves he is making, and the particular pitch he is working, that he has neither time nor interest in fear or looking down. Why look down when you want to go up?

Equipment for Rock Climbing

Your dress and equipment are different from those you need for scrambling or climbing. Consider the following:

1 When starting to learn on the 10–12ft boulder, keep your hair short or tie it back Apache-fashion. You do not want it falling in your eyes at the moment when you have a split-second decision to make.
2 If you are ascending larger slopes, wear a helmet of BSI specifications. Avoid cheap Continental imitations.
3 The usual gear is a warm sweater/pullover over a shirt or string vest.
4 Any trousers will do. Wear molecords or good worsteds for longer climbs, but jeans or any loose-fitting trousers that allow the legs to bend easily will suffice for short climbs, say up to 100ft (30m).
5 Rock-climbing boots are different to other climbing boots. PAs (Pierre Alains), Gollies, RDs, and various others are available. They are all variations of lightweight, usually canvas-topped, footwear with slightly stiffened rubber soles. Training shoes are commonly used. If you have to do some ordinary climbing to reach the crag destined for the rock climb, wear ordinary mountain boots and change into the lightweights to go up the crag. Austrians use felt-soled Kletterschuhe, and the French and Italians favour rope-soled espadrilles or scarpetti. Unless you are resident in such an area, however, it is rarely worth while letting some guide (probably on commis-

sion) talk you into buying the local brand.

6 Wet socks are carried, usually in a trouser pocket or in the belt, to be slipped over footwear when you come to a wet patch, where the rubber soles might slip too easily.

7 In addition to the close contact the thinner boots allow with the rockface, you need all the feel that your feet can give you, so cut your toenails short. By the same token, and for convenience, cut your fingernails short too.

8 Rock climbers carry a watch in the pocket, never on the wrist.

9 Do wear a good strong leather belt, for there are a number of things you need to carry on it.

10 A climbing harness is needed for longer climbs but seldom for short ones. It passes over the shoulders and under the crutch, and is laced across the chest and round the waist. It connects up with the ropes used, and prevents a sudden strain and jerk from damaging internal organs by distributing the shock pull power of a fall, etc.

11 See the special section on rope (p 73). Even a medium or short rock climb may call for a rope, and one of the advantages of going with a couple of friends is that the cost of buying a rope can be split up between you. If a rope after a year or so begins to look badly frayed or cut in some places by rock edges, it is cheaper and kinder to your friends and relatives not to risk it for main belays, etc.

12 You will certainly need some rope (or tape) slings, if not both, with some chockstones on them (see below), and some pitons, Karabiners, etc. Their use is explained later (p 96). Half a dozen Karabiners, the same number of slings and four or five metal chockstones suffice for an average ascent. If you are in a party with two or three fairly good rock climbers but have no guide or experienced man who has done the rockface before, make sure you have a proper guidebook or leaflet about that particular face – preferably one using the internationally accepted conventional signs.

How Difficult is the Climb?

A Welsh climber, Owen Glynne-Jones, instituted a distinct standard of climbs, but at the most these can be merely a rough guide as to what you should expect, for the following reasons:

1 What is easy to one climber may be difficult to another.

2 What is a good scramble in summer may be a difficult climb in winter.

3 Mountain surfaces alter within a few years. A landslide, an avalanche, a long

A good rope is an invaluable aid on any rock face

wet summer, or severe freezing in winter can change the holds or destroy them.

4 Frequent climbing of favourite rockfaces may wear out the holds. What the compiler of the guidebook knew as good solid square holds may now be nail-scratched flakes on which you hang by hope and prayer.

Some years back I was climbing with a famous man who assured me the climb was merely *difficult* – it said so in the guidebook. To my anxiety I found the climb far more exhausting than that, but he dismissed my anxieties, although I noticed he too found it exhausting. I later found out that his guidebook had been published in 1920, and he had never changed it! Prompted by curiosity I examined a modern guidebook, which listed the climb as severe. Erosion often wears away good holds, making climbs harder.

The Glynne-Jones scale runs as follows, in ascending order of difficulty: Easy (E), Moderate (Mod), Difficult (Diff), Very Difficult (VD), Severe (S), and Very Severe (VS).

Another weakness of the gradations lies in the fact that one climber may use more artificial aids than another, and to him the rockface is naturally less strenuous to ascend. Generally speaking, on an international scale, the words in the scale above are replaced by numbers I, II, III, IV, V, VI, each of which can be preceded by a plus or a minus symbol as a more precise classification. If the climb is essentially made with artificial aids, another international system – A1, A2, A3, A4 – comes into use, the letter e being added if expansion bolts are used, as in A2e, for example. One important use of the standards above is to hinder wise rock climbers from tackling a face that is totally beyond their experience.

The Technique of Rock Climbing

Your First Rock Climb

Do not go alone. Take somebody with you, even if he or she is not trying to climb. Preferably climb where other climbers are to be found. You can ask for advice if you need it, or for help if required.

Now check the rock. Does it flake away in your hands? Does it crumble? (Please do not climb on chalk, it is very bad.) If it is solid, go ahead; if not, leave it alone. Where possible, find rock where there is

NOTE:
* HANDS USED FOR BALANCE
* TOES BALANCED ON ROCK
* BODY AWAY FROM ROCK FACE

* BODY WELL BACK FROM THE ROCK FACE
* TOES LIGHTLY BALANCED
* HANDS FIRMLY HOLDING BALANCE

an easy way off, in case you find the first try too exhausting. Anyway, try again; we all know what that first attempt is like.

Find a rock not more than three times your own height, for most people can jump down twice their own height without injuring themselves. Now check the ground you might have to jump on to ensure there are no broken boulders, no bottles or other objects that could cause a sprained ankle. If there are, clear the ground in case you need to jump. We never jump down unless absolutely necessary, so work out in advance whether you can climb down more or less the way you went up – if there is no easy way off. We will assume that you have one piton attached to your belt. This will come in handy if you have, to pause and 'garden' a hold. Now 'gardening' is avoided by climbers but it is essential for the beginner. If you find a hold that is overgrown by moss or grass, or filled with pebbles, steady yourself with three limbs and use one hand, and your piton, to clear the hold. Scrape down to the bare rock, making it safe to step upon: many handholds of this moment become the footholds of the next.

If you find that a hold comes loose in your hands, let it fall, shouting 'Below!' to warn others. Then see whether you can scrape a hold with your piton. If not, make a sideways traverse, move crablike across the rock, and somewhere or other you are bound to find another hold – unless you are on the Eiger North Wall, and as a beginner you ought not to be there.

Here is a tip that very few instructors ever remember to tell the beginner: when you start rock climbing, your shoes may be wet from grass, heather or moss you have walked across to get to your boulder/ rockface. Rub the soles on an old sock, or anything to dry off the moisture. Dry soles hold the small places on the rock best.

Your hands are mainly for balancing, your feet for climbing. Keep the heels low, and do not reach for high handholds, which disturb the balance of the foot. Beginners often try to reach up too high and so disturb their balance on the rock.

THE WAY DOWN

Let us first deal with the jump, just in case. 'Look before you leap' – here the old proverb comes into its own. There is also a psychological advantage in knowing where you expect to land; it helps you feel that you are in control of yourself, which is very important. The only other point is to remember to twist your body outwards, so that you are facing away from the rock. That prevents you from falling backwards. Keep both feet close together, and let the muscles go limp. Try not to jump – ever. However difficult it is to climb down, it is less risky than a jump. Beginners must know how to jump, however, but remember not to jump more than twice your own height.

If the rock allows it, make the first move of your descent sideways. Be sure that you can spot three holds before you slide over the edge to go down, so that you know roughly what the first three moves will be. Find a good foothold first, then a handhold not more than 2ft (61cm) below that, and so on. Never try too big a step. The beginner experiences an illusion that a foothold is very far down when in fact it is seldom more than a couple of feet; this is because the eyes are 4–5ft (1·23–1·5m) further away from that hold than are the feet. Seek your handholds about hip height when coming down; try not to reach below that, for it is difficult to do so without losing a foothold, especially for beginners. The beginner finds it difficult to allow the bodyweight to descend below handholds, but it gets easier with practice.

You have most control when facing the rock, especially on descent (Figure 12). Here you can see the type of footholds in profile. There is no indication of their width or depth, but since you should not expect to remain on any one for any length of time, this is not so important.

HANDHOLDS

It is neither practical nor logical to illustrate all handholds. They are made basically on the same profiles as footholds, but there are different ways in which the hands can hold the rock.

1 Have you ever climbed a ladder? Of course, and your hands performed one simple *pull up*; the fingers curled over the bit higher up and balanced you while you shifted your foot. We do not use this to hoist ourselves up, for climbing is done best with the feet.
2 The *Underpull* reminds us that hands are used for balance, the fingers of the hand performing the same movement as described above, but the hand gripping the rock so that the palm faces you (not so difficult to imagine if you think that the piece of rock may be jutting out slightly to the side of your route).

THE WRONG WAY

* CLIMBER GLUED TO
  THE ROCK
* CANNOT SEE WHERE
  TO PLACE HIS FEET
* ARMS TOO HIGH
* NO BALANCE!

THE SAFE WAY

* BODY WELL BACK FROM
  THE ROCK SO THAT CLIMBER
  CAN SEE WHERE
  HIS FEET ARE GOING.
* ARMS NOT HIGHER
  THAN THE SHOULDERS
* GOOD BALANCE

66

3 The *push up* exerts pressure on the rock, just like the push-up exercises loved by gym instructors. The palm of the hand is pushed down on the surface of rock.

4 The *finger grip* is useful on a rounded or horizontal ledge that is not deep enough or incut sufficiently for the whole hand to curl round it. It is a hold requiring a good foothold.

5 The *side grip* is useful when going round a corner of rock. One of the climbs on Lliwedd (Wales) is noted for the side grips required.

6 With the *jug handle* the whole hand can grip firmly, as if it were gripping the handle of a milk jug. The 'handle' rises from the main body of the rock.

7 In the *under grip* the hand is turned over, fingers pointing upwards; it is quite sufficient to maintain balance.

8 There is one special movement called mantelshelf, and this reminds me of the golden rule for all rock climbers, climbers and scramblers: 'You must be strong enough, and sufficiently practised to pull your entire bodyweight up by your arms alone.'

JAMMING

This technique has added a great deal to rock climbing, because it has enabled otherwise impracticable climbs to be made. Jamming is very successful on gritstone, and good on granite and some sandstones. It is best performed with fingerless gloves on to take the strain of rough-edged rock on the flesh. You may know the feeling of getting stuck in something, and jamming is the art of deliberately sticking in a narrow aperture of rock in order to balance yourself. You may ask how you get out again. The answer is feet first. There is a narrow crack and you put your foot in it, and twisting the foot either to left or right, which ever is more comfortable. It is essential to do the twist, because remembering which way you twisted the foot to get it in makes it possible to twist it the other way to get it out. Many such cracks on a mountain are narrower at the bottom than at the top, and the very act of moving upwards releases pressure on the part trapped by the jam, this is more obvious when the knee is pushed in for a hold in this manner. Jamming with feet or knees is not so precise as with hands, fists and fingers.

Shoulders, elbows and arms can also be used for a jam. With the novice, provided he does not panic, it is possible to lever the limb out of the hold easily by reversing the movements by which it was inserted.

Hands and fingers are the most favoured jams. Although the flesh can be roughed up by the rock, the method gives a fairly secure purchase for balance. The fingers can be put into a crack in three ways, the best way by turning the hand upside down and the easiest way by placing it in naturally; the third method is to place the thumb across the palm of the hand to thicken the size of the jamming hand. Most of the holds for jamming are side holds, but some can be used for a vertical pull-up; the best for this is the jammed fist, which is inserted, clenched and can then be used to haul up the body weight. Completely relax the hand to withdraw it.

Friction Holds

Gritstone, some sandstone, granite and rhyolite allow some good holds by sheer friction. Hand, arm, or foot are pressed against the rock face, and held long enough to allow movement to some other hold.

Layback Climbing

This should not be attempted unless you are in good condition and have really strong arms, for they must carry not only your entire weight but also the pressure you exert against them. Take hold of the crack with both hands, one above the other; lean backwards, extending the arms full length; swing both feet up high, one above the other on the opposing rock surface; and start walking up it like a monkey climbing a tree. The hands must keep pace with the feet; every time a hand moves a foot moves too. Never hang about, get moving, stay moving, and relieve your arms of the strain quickly. If the feet are not kept high up, you will just slide off the rock.

Grooves

Sometimes you will find the rock split open at a wide angle, almost like the pages of this book as you read it, and occasionally as smooth as the page itself. There is quite a good way to tackle this sort of rock. You reach with one hand only at a time, the feet pressing outwards, one on either side of the angle, and the remaining hand pressing down hard on the best hold it can find. Do not reach up too high; keep handholds lower than shoulder height as a general rule. Sometimes with one foot on a good hold you can balance the other with a purely frictional hold. You are now bridging the gap between the two angled surfaces with your straddled legs. Do not be afraid to push your legs outwards against the rock. Unless it is an exceptionally good hold, do not reach the arm above the shoulders during this manoeuvre. If you tire, you can find a good foothold somewhere and place both feet on it, then lean out and balance the arms against the other angled surface. Keep hand-pressure holds low.

The Beginner's Commonest Error

This is searching all the time for handholds. When you cannot find a good handhold, seek for another foothold, perhaps only inches above where your feet are placed now, and from there you may find a good handhold.

Sideways to the Top

This heading sounds like a Rocky Mountain Indian saying, but it is in fact a description of traversing. Every rock climber should practise this, the art of moving sideways across the rockface, for it can save your life as well as enabling you to make a better climb. One rule: the moving foot always goes between the resting foot and the rockface. Use your hands alone if you can see a good foothold just beyond the present one, making sure you have a solid purchase with your hands. Then swing across, stretching out the leg nearest the sought-after foothold; when you do this, you change your usual stance, and for once press the knees against the rock for a frictional purchase. This is an exception to the rule that you should keep your knees away from the rock, to see where your feet are going. When traversing, think of footholds all the time, and make sure each one is a solid one, so that you can rest if need be. During this sideways moving it is quite legitimate to lift your feet up to a higher line of the ridge or ledges, and a practised climber can easily swing a leg up almost to waist level to continue his progress.

Climbing a Crack

This may be done partly by jamming holds using shoulder, knee, feet and fist, or, if the crack is very narrow, by the layback method.

The art is to use any holds on either corner of the crack (outside it), in addition to the jamming techniques. It is one of the harder things for a beginner to face, because the psychological approach is often inhibited by the feeling it cannot be done. But it is done, every day.

CLIMBING A CORNER

A groove is not so much a right-angle, and both sides are wider than those of a corner, but the methods used are much the same. Essentially some bridging will be used (see Chimneys, below), as well as some jamming, and maybe also some traversing from one side to another. The main error of beginners is to search for handholds more than good footholds. Remember you can pause to recover your breath and think on a good foothold, but never with a good handhold alone.

CHIMNEYS

A narrow chimney can be climbed by pressing the back against one wall of it and alternate knees against the other, balancing with arms, elbows or shoulders.

Two other methods are possible and are described below. The first is bridging, by which you place one foot on one wall, the other on the wall facing it, while balancing with the hands on the two walls; you then raise one hand and one foot, one hand, one foot, and progress in this way. This method is only useful when the wall surfaces are rough enough to provide some good holds. The second method, the smoother backing up, is the best way to tackle a smooth-walled chimney. You press your back against the smoother wall, and push the feet against the opposite wall, placing the palms of the hands on the rock in the natural position where they hang, just below your back. You move the hands up a few inches at a time, then shift one foot up, followed by the other. The secret is to keep your feet as horizontal as you can, pressing them hard. You may find the chimney is widening as you get to the top, so you turn inwards, one foot slightly higher than the other, and when you feel secure, you make the movement into a bridging one, pressing hard until your lowered foot finds the hold you have spotted for it. From the bridging position you can move on to one wall and climb up. Maybe the chimney remains more or less the same width all the way to the top, and you realise that you are only a move from the top. You want to know then how to get out of it.

If the chimney narrows, you would probably finish up doing a knee and arm technique, but if the aperture is constant, one way is to press the feet hard against the opposite rock, balance with one palm against the rock and then feel with the other for a good handhold, preferably a solid jug handle. Keep the feet pressing tightly against the opposite wall while your hand reaches up for a hold; then you can search with one foot for a foothold, or reverse the hands, turn in towards the rock, and haul yourself over the ledge. Most chimneys are either narrower at the top or wider at the top, so this technique is seldom necessary. Occasionally you can just lift yourself out backwards.

Stuck in the Chimney

If you encounter a boulder or rock that is acting as a giant chockstone, you would be wise to go on climbing past it. Always test the stone with one hand, gingerly. The last thing you want is to have it fall on you. Never grip a chockstone as a support unless it is so blocked that it cannot roll round or fall.

Move deeper in or further out of the chimney as you feel it necessary. Frictional holds are better deeper inside. Never put your back to a wall that bends inwards further up. If the walls are obviously wet or mossy, put wet socks over your rock-shoes. Chimneys are fairly good to climb in wet weather, being naturally protected against the elements.

Gullies

These are invariably a line of descent for water from the mountain, and are often damp and mossy, with greasy rocks. The main hazard is the presence of small loose stones. The techniques vary from bridging, backing up, and jamming to straight climbing on one wall or the other. They are wider than chimneys for the most part.

Loose Rock

The climber has always to be concerned with the solidity of the rock upon which he is making his moves. Limestone, sandstone and quartz-bearing rocks usually show it when they are loose. Their texture can be felt by the hand and sometimes seen by the eye. When you are on other rock, take a Karabiner and tap it, or bang away with a foot or a fist. If the rock sounds solid, there is not much risk, but should your ear detect any hollow ring about it, find another hold. If in doubt about the reliability of the rock, be much more careful about each move, ensure that your weight and balance are equally distributed on three limbs while exploring with the fourth, and take your time.

OVERHANGS

There are overhangs of varying sharpness of angle. Some are easy, others not, and this depends upon the type of rock and the holds offered. They are not for a beginner without experience, but there comes a time when you feel ready to tackle one, so start with a bulge at the top rather than something like Kilnsey Crag (Yorkshire). You must observe the following points:

1 Check the route before you go up it, because you cannot retreat. The best you could manage might be a sideways traverse, but this is not to be recommended.
2 The body is kept almost at right-angles to the overhang rockface, and the feet press into the rock with the body weight.
3 You must take as good a hold as you can with both hands, and pull upwards. Then bend the leg in towards you, and put it on a higher position. The overhangs usually have roughish surfaces, so when you have balanced with that foot, move the other up to balance; press the feet against the rock, seek hold with your hands, and so on.
4 Obviously you must be roped and belayed by friends while you experience this thrill. One of the friends must be sufficiently expert to help you.
5 Move as quickly as possible, for this technique places inordinate strain on the arms, and this is increased by the psychological strain.
6 The higher up the feet are angled on the rock, the less will be the strain on the arms.
7 You must always wear a helmet when climbing an overhang.

7 Rope

The legend of Damocles tells how a king sat below a sword which was suspended by a single thread. Like him, we must understand that our lives may depend upon the rope we use. Regardless of cost, do not buy or use secondhand ropes. Heed the following grim warning:

> This is the tale of Sammy Shand
> Who bought his ropes all secondhand,
> Not knowing that inside they'd frayed,
> And so poor Sammy was dismayed
> When on an ice ledge he was trapped
> Just at the time his leadrope snapped,
> He fell far, flying round and round,
> And plunged into a deep *Bergschrund*.
> In that crevasse is Sammy's grave,
> The cost of burial was all he saved.

A good guidebook will usually tell you how much rope you need for a specific climb, but as a general rule the minimum lengths are 60ft (18m) for two climbers and 100ft (30m) for three climbers. If you can carry it easily, take 120ft (36·6m) at all times when rope is needed.

I have no hesitation in advising climbers going to Switzerland or Austria to take British ropes with them. Continental ropes are often insufficiently tested, but British ropes are subjected to British Standards regulations (BSI35/3104), so that they have been thoroughly and scientifically tested. Many Swiss still use comparatively dangerous plaited hemp or cheap sisal ropes, which have little elasticity, can rot easily from the inside of the rope outwards, and are very treacherous. Professor John Clements tells the story of reaching a certain overhang where some club had left a permanent rope fixed to the mountain. It seemed frayed and thoroughly suspect. 'Is that rope reliable?' he asked.

'Of course', was the Swiss guide's reply, 'that rope has been blessed by the Pope himself!'

QUALITIES NEEDED IN ROPE

It must be strong enough to absorb the force of a falling body, which is much heavier than that of a still body. In a fall one can weigh ten times in exertive force what one would weigh standing still. A good safe rope stretches as it progressively absorbs the energy generated by a fall, like the hydraulic action of automobile brakes.

Rope must be tough enough not to snap or cut on a rough or jagged piece of rock. It must be light enough not to become an awkward burden while you are climbing. Provided that you have a good BSI rope, your main problems concern the balance between elasticity and weight. It goes without saying that you want a rope that is easy and comfortable to handle, and not rough on hands that are cold and wet. Remember that the higher the mountain, the more likely it is that there will be wet snow or at least moisture towards the top. Swiss hemp or manila ropes can become stiff and unbearable to handle when wet or frozen.

TYPES OF ROPE

There are few things without some disadvantage to balance up their good points, and so it is with rope. It is wise, therefore, to know what you are going to use it for before you buy it. The best rope for general purposes is nylon (BSI 3104), which is light and supple, with a very good capacity to absorb shock and sudden strain. It does not absorb water to any great degree, is as pleasant to handle when soaking wet or frozen as when dry, cannot be damaged by rot or mildew, and, if properly cared for, will last a long time.

On the negative side nylon must be kept away from chemicals, petrol and car-battery acid, and it may cut if swung to and fro across a sharp piece of rock for any length of time (this is usually avoidable). The melting point is c 250°C (or 484°F), and if one piece of nylon runs out across another under the pressure of a falling load, it can set up a

Lord of all he surveys, this climber is safe in the knowledge that he is well roped-up

frictional heat that could approach the melting point. So care must be taken in managing the ropes. German, Austrian and Swiss ropes can also be found in artificial fibres, but these are often difficult to tie; the knots do not hold well because their ropes are usually of the kernmantel type (which has fibres running down the whole length of a rope, usually inside colourful woven sheaths). They lack the flexibility and stability of the British products, but are often better against abrasion and less subject to twisting.

Never use steel wire rope when climbing. Rescue teams occasionally use it for getting a casualty out of a crevasse or other difficulty, but that is a highly specialised use.

British-style cable (hawser) has the fibres safely twisted in strands, of which three are twisted to form the rope; this gives added protection against fraying and snapping. The fact that the strands are twisted adds to the extension power of the rope as a whole, and makes it very shock-resistant.

Manila and hemp ropes are also covered by a BSI certificate (2052) to guarantee that they have been passed as rot-proof and of a good quality. I invariably use one of these ropes – ¾in for waist lines or an abseil belay sling – the advantage being that nylon against nylon can quickly burn through and melt, whereas nylon against manila or hemp will not.

THICKNESS

For general purposes BSI nylon 3104 no 4 ⅜in cable rope is excellent on rock, snow, crevasse rescue work, main belays and for runners. If abseiling, double it.

BSI 3104 no 3 1¼in is lighter to carry. It can be used double on rock climbs and single for most snow climbs, and makes a good top rope used single and a good abseil rope doubled. But it is not so good as a main belay rope.

HOW TO HANDLE ROPES

1 Keep the rope clean, shake stones and grit free from it after each climb.
2 Dry ropes only in a warm dry room, never in artificial heat and never near a fire or stove.
3 Open out a rope to dry it out. Never leave a wet rope coiled, or mildew and

rope can rot it (manila or hemp) or lessen its springiness (nylon). Try to use fresh arid air to dry it.

4 Keep all rope away from sunlight or artificial light when you store it.

5 Never tread on a rope, especially if wearing crampons.

6 Never drag or twist ropes along a rock surface, or ice or snow ridges.

7 Keep nylon ropes away from all chemicals (especially if you carry it in a car boot with battery and spare petrol can).

8 Never use any chemical to clean a rope.

9 Never use a climbing rope for any other purpose until it is too old to use for climbing.

Is Your Rope Still Safe?

Any used rope will have a few small frayed or snapped strands. All rope that comes into contact with a climber, or with other rope, has some abrasions. Check how deep they are, and whether they encircle the rope. If not, your eyes will tell you whether it is still safe. Loose yarns deep cuts in the strand signify that the rope is unsafe for mountain work.

Open up the cable to inspect the inside condition of the strands. See whether grit or stones are embedded in them, and whether such foreign bodies have cut fibres or strands.

Any signs of chemical corrosion on the rope mean that it is finished. In addition, if there are signs that the nylon strands have melted together anywhere, the rope has been too near heat, and as such has lost its elasticity and tensile strength. Even a small fusion of fibres may mean the entire length of rope has been made brittle.

Manila or hemp rope is very easily subject to mildew or rot from damp in between the strands. Internal wear is speeded up by grit or stones having worked their way inside.

If ever in doubt, buy new ropes.

Rope Techniques

When it is not in use, keep the rope coiled. Coil your rope one half turn to the left, then one half turn to the right, for every circle you make. This method prevents it twisting. You may use a friend's arms or your own foot and knee to help coil the rope in this way. Carry rope slung across one shoulder and under the other arm, or attached to the shoulder and the waist, and carried on the back by loops.

Waist Rope

1 If you are not wearing a webbing waistband, use a separate length of rope for the waist – this is your insurance against falls.
2 The waist rope or band must be broad enough in effect not to bite into the body if there is a fall. Even so a body left unconscious dangling on a rope can suffer severe damage within 20 minutes, as circulation may be cut off, and damage to the spine ensue.
3 The waist fastening must be sufficiently tight not to slip off over the hips if one falls upside down.
4 Many rock climbers favour harness, usually of artificial fibre webbing, which is designed to distribute the points of strain, usually between the waist and the chest.
5 For artificial climbs (where the ascent is made at some peril with practically no holds but pegs, etc) and especially for all very difficult and severe climbs, a special harness with a loop over the shoulder and another round the opposite thigh offers greater protection.
6 All rock climbing and some other climbs should only be undertaken with ropes attached correctly to each climber's waist rope or harness.

How to Tie Up

1 To avoid friction of rope against rope, always use a Karabiner (see p 96). Remember that nylon can melt if violent movement sets up friction.
2 Check the position of the Krab (Karabiner) gate; it should be facing away from you, and the sleeve should be screwed down as soon as you are on the rope. Krabs offer the quick method of release, for they do not freeze solid as a rope knot might.
3 Attach rope to Krab by a Tarbuck-type knot.
4 I was taught to knot each turn of a waist rope every time I twisted it round my body. Some people use seven turns, others five or three. It depends upon the rope, the climb and you, but you do not want so many that it becomes impossible to attach the Karabiner.

Know the Ropes

Many a fall is turned into a harmless slip because of the rope. Ropes properly used add to your safety; badly used they add to your difficulties. The best of rope will not prevent negligence or stupidity bringing disaster. Practise your knots and rope technique regularly before you go climbing on ascents where ropes are essential.

THE TARBUCK KNOT

THE FIGURE-OF-EIGHT KNOT

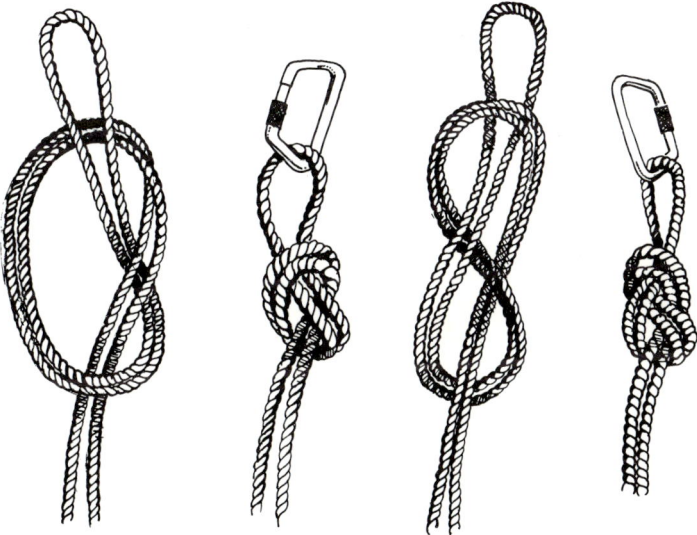

BELAYING

As a ship uses an anchor to avoid coming adrift, so a climber uses a belay, but the climber can better the ship by using a running belay, which enables him to move but still gives him some protection. Note the following points:

1 A belay must be well done – if not, it is useless.
2 No book can teach you how to find secure belays, but it can supply some pointers. Personal experience is necessary.
3 The secret of a good belay is a sound anchorage, from which the rope comes to the belayer, who is there to take the first shock and strain in case of a slip.
4 Wherever possible, locate the anchorage above the waist level of the belayer; this is a simple rule, but neglected only by the unwise. If necessary, sit to achieve the upward angle from your waist to the anchorage, bracing the feet as you normally would if standing.
5 Never overload a belay, or an anchorage. One climber at a time please!
6 Belay ropes should be kept slightly taut, like a good fishing line, so that the belayer can feel the movements of the man he is helping to climb.
7 Taut rope also lessens the chance of the belayer being pulled off his stance by accidental movement, which is possible when the rope is slack.

ANCHORAGES

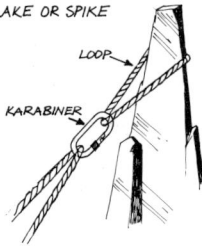

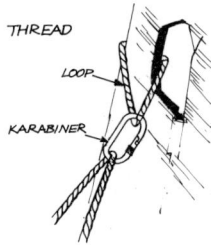

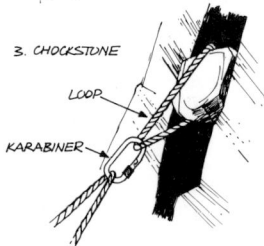

N B SEE ALSO ILLUSTRATIONS OF PITONS

8 There is one good rule of thumb for beginners to judge whether a rock is going to make a good anchorage behind their belay – do you think it is sound enough to rope down a man who is injured? If not, forget it.

9 All men and women take risks, but to even out the odds you must add to your adventurousness a basic knowledge of techniques to justify the risks. Remember this when belaying.

ANCHORAGES FOR BELAYERS

The following techniques should be employed when establishing a belay in connection with a good anchorage:

1 Take a good hold, making sure you can balance well.

2 Fix your sling round, over or through the anchorage, as needs be.

3 If the rock is very rough or jagged, it may be necessary to use a leather sleeve or patch to protect the rope from movement against the rock that might cause fraying or cutting. A guide or guidebook would advise you if the rock is this rough.

4 You need a Karabiner, usually one with a breaking strain of not less than 5,000lb (2,270kg). Keep the gate away from the rock, and screw the sleeve shut once it is on the sling.

5 The anchorage should be above your waist line (even if you sit to achieve this).

6 The rope on which the no 2 climber ascends is called the action rope. It is passed through the Karabiner on the anchorage sling, and the end is fastened by a figure eight knot to the Karabiner on the belayer's belt (waist rope).

7 A 2ft 6in (75cm) loop is pulled through the waistband karabiner. With this loop you make another figure eight knot. Step close into the anchorage rock while you do this, so that the rope between you and the rock is really taut (making you safer). The figure eight knot is fastened on the top of your waistband karabiner, leaving a free loop of 12–18in (30·5–45·7cm) as an expendable reserve hanging down harmlessly behind you. Once this is tied, you step forward to the original position.

8 Put on leather gloves, which you need for handling rope.

9 Check that both Karabiner gates are covered by screw sleeves.

10 Take a good stance, with your feet well braced against the rock. In ninety-nine cases out of a hundred you will not have to withstand the shock of a slip below, but you always stand prepared for it. Even if sitting, brace the feet. Remember that the belayer seeks to minimise strain on the anchorage.

11 Place the rope over the shoulder opposite to that on which the climber is coming upwards; the hand holding the rope that side twists the rope through

the hand over the wrist – it will not take the strain but it makes the rope easier to control. The rope passes under the armpit on the side nearest the climber, and is pulled in until it is taut enough to detect the climber's movements.

Practice makes perfect. Several clubs and climbing schools have places where you can practise belaying with a sack of sand – if not, try it out with a loaded rucksack – before you risk your friend's weight. In dangerous and very exposed places it is common to make two anchorages to protect the belayer, who stands like the tail of a letter Y between them.

The beginner can also benefit by the use of webbing slings or rope slings with coloured strands. This makes identification of the parts easier.

Running Belays

The method described above is good when you climb from A to B, and your friend follows you up. The subsequent notes explain the method of making your way up a longer pitch, while lessening the chance of a serious fall. Beginners must realise that every time you slip on rock you are not necessarily in any danger – unless you are not belayed properly.

This type of belay is commonly effected by pitons (see p 90) and what serve as such. At every piton a Karabiner is needed. The number of pitons and Karabiners required must be known or estimated, and a couple of spares added. If there is a fall, the rope will stretch (this is good), and the idea is to limit the depth that you fall. Hence, where running belays are required for rock climbing (winter climbs too), they are seldom placed at more than 20ft (6m) apart.

Always face the climber when handling rope. Do not face inwards to the rock when you are waiting for the second to climb, but if you are the second man protecting your leader, face inwards to the rock. In brief, always face the way that covers the climber.

When the leader is climbing, the second man can protect him by keeping control of his rope, and resisting an upward pull caused by a leader's slip. (If a leader falls, the rope through a running belay would pull the second man upwards). In some cases it is essential for the second man to be belayed to an anchorage himself in order to give better resistance to a leader climbing with running belays.

The second man always watches the leader's every move, feeding rope slowly and carefully as the leader climbs. Remember to be ready to feed rope quickly after a short stop – while the leader checks the pitch ahead, after which he may make several quick decisive steps to reach a more secure stance.

When a leader is placing running belays, the second man should be able to follow him, extracting the pitons, etc, as he goes, without wandering far from the original route followed by the leader. A good leader is aware of the potential of his second (and subsequent) climber, and places running belays where it would increase the confidence of others – although the leader may not need them himself.

Remember to remove the pitons if you are the last man up. The leader protecting a second uses the shoulder belay described above. The second protecting the leader uses the waist belay. The waist belay differs from the shoulder belay only in that the rope is held just above the waist line round the back instead of over one shoulder.

Roping Down

The most experienced climber goes last, because this is hardest. The least experienced goes first, protected from above, and by running belays which (if you knew you were going back that way) you would have left in position. It is more difficult to retrieve pitons going down. Remember, always remember, an abandoned piton and/or Karabiner are worth less than losing your life or injuring yourself (see also Abseiling, p 85).

Warning to the Foolhardy

Some climbers are afflicted by a desire to show off or to chance their arm by skipping out on belays. This is not fair to the climbers who must follow them.

> Here is the tale of boastful B. Day
> Who never used a running belay,
> He said: It looks easy, I'll trust to luck.
> B was carried away by an ambulance truck.

What To Do When a Fall Occurs

If the second man is protected by the leader but falls, on an average pitch he becomes a static weight whose load barely exceeds his own normal bodyweight. The leader braces strongly against the rock and controls the belay rope, being well supported by the anchorage behind him, and in most cases the fall is checked easily. No 2 takes hold of the rockface, steadies himself and carries on climbing, either up or down; and buys his leader a couple of beers next time they are at the pub.

The further the leader falls when protected by the second man, the greater the dynamic force over and above his own bodyweight becomes. The second who is protecting him must not panic, but tighten slowly the wrist in which the rope is twisted, and slowly fold his arms across the body, increasing the friction of the rope around his own body; this slows down the rope's movement. No 2 braces himself against being pulled up by the upward force of the rope (on the other end of which the leader is falling). If a second man knows he is, say, not more than 10ft (3m) above ground, and if the ground is level, with no boulders or any obstruction to damage his feet or ankles, he can save a falling leader from a nasty accident if they are on rough jagged rocks by jumping down himself, while holding the rope tight. This at once arrests the leader's downward flight. Be careful to do everything possible to prevent a fallen leader swinging against the rocks and injuring himself.

In all notes on rope techniques where there is reference to the second man, this means that climber moving up to a leader belayed, or that climber who is belayed below to protect a man going up. It has nothing to do with the number of climbers in a party.

Clear Communication

During rock climbs with rope, communication is essential to avoid stupid mistakes. If all climbers use the same phrases, the probability of error is obviously reduced.

The first man up is called the leader. While he is climbing, he pauses and fixes a running belay. He calls down to the second, who is protecting him, 'Runner on', meaning 'I'm going to move again; here is the new fulcrum of force.' He finishes his planned pitch of the climb, and calls out, 'I'm there.' But the second man does not release his own safety belay before he feels the leader haul in enough rope for it to go taut, which the leader signals by the shout, 'Taking in'. When the second feels the rope is taut, and can see it is not snagged but hangs free, he replies, 'That's me'.

The leader makes sure of his anchorage, adjusts his belay, makes certain his leather gloves are on, and then calls out, 'When you're ready'. Now the second answers, 'Climbing'. There is now a double check call, 'Okay'.

If the climber feels the rope is too tight – he has perhaps made a wrong move, and must descend, or go sideways, needing more rope – he shouts, 'Slack'. The leader releases more rope. Later during the climb the man may make several fast moves in succession, and if the rope does not move fast enough, he calls out, 'Take her in'.

Perhaps there is a gust of wind at an awkward moment, or a slight error. The climber shouts, 'Hold it'. At once the leader hauls in fast, bracing his feet against the rock, and a disaster is averted. Never neglect your communications. To climb a rockface without signals is stupid.

ABSEILING

There are some rockfaces it is inadvisable to climb down, and some conditions, such as a sudden worsening of weather, when it becomes imperative to get down the quickest way possible. The answer is to rope down, which is known as abseiling. This is exciting, fast and quite safe, provided it has been practised beforehand. It is fairly safe where there has been no previous practice, as long as the abseiler can discipline himself to follow instructions precisely, concentrate upon what he is doing and keep calm.

The rope on which the descent is to be made is doubled, and it is attached by sling – either to a solid rock spike, piton, etc, only after the anchorage has been thoroughly checked for safety. A piton must be driven into a horizontal crack, for obvious reasons; vertical or diagonal cracks will not be able to give much security or support at all. If there is no single good anchorage use several, so that if one lets go, the others will hold.

The two lengths of the rope are lowered over the edge carefully so that they do not become twisted. The wind may move them, but try

The excitement of abseiling down a tricky face in worsening conditions

to keep them as near the area of landing as possible.

Never use a worn sling to make the anchorage. A good webbing sling is far better than most rope slings. If the rock round which the sling is placed to hold the abseil rope is jagged or otherwise rough, use either a leather patch or some handkerchiefs to protect the sling from friction against the torn surface. The higher the sling is placed, the easier it is to go over the edge on the abseil rope. The lower the sling, the more psychologically disturbing it is, for the beginner especially.

The anchorage should be such that it is possible to haul the rope down after the operation is complete. Check to see whether any spur of rock could snag the rope during the hauling down. Where possible a safety rope should be fastened to another anchorage, natural or piton, and joined by Karabiner to the abseiler's waist webbing or rope. This gives confidence to those doing an abseil for the first time.

If you are the abseiler, stand across the rope, so that it lies on the ground between your outstretched legs. You are facing the anchorage, and proceed as follows:

1 Grasp the rope in front of you with your left hand, and the rope behind you with your right hand. Wind it carefully over your head, so that the rope reposes on the left shoulder, then let go with your right hand and pick up the rope with that hand again, so that the rope is held with both palms facing outwards, the way you are looking. The rope from the anchorage is passed round the back of the right thigh, and across the front, over the left shoulder. It is held behind by the right hand, and in front by the left. The left hand is chin high as you move backwards down over the edge, but takes a natural lower position during the actual descent.

2 Keep the feet flat against the rockface, keep in contact with the rock and avoid any suggestion of free swinging.

3 Never grasp the rope too tightly with the upper hand – this left hand is required for balance only.

4 Do not be put off by the fact that the moving rope bites with heavy friction into the back of your thigh, chest and left shoulder; it lasts only a short time, but do expect some minor discomfort.

5 When abseiling, never let the feet get wide apart. Make simple small steps. Keep the legs fairly close together in order to keep the rope between the legs locked in position, with the rope as high up at the top of the thigh as you can keep it. If the rope should slip to knee level you may lose control.

6 Lean well back from the rockface so that you can see where you are going, and remember to take all the strain of your weight on the right, controlling hand. Keep front of body to rockface when the going is steep or vertical. When the going is not so sheer and dizzy, you may turn slightly so that the left side of your body faces the rock.

7 To slow down during abseil bring the right hand holding the rope normally behind you to the front of the body, holding fast. The rope then makes more contact with your body clothing, and this friction slows down the descent.

Another method of abseiling utilises a wide webbed sling. You twist

the sling by a simple turn in the middle, and step into the two halves, one leg in each. A screwgate Karabiner is used to join the sling to your waist band. The abseil rope is on the ground, and you stand astride it while it is put through the Karabiner, which joins loop and waistband, over the left shoulder. Then, left hand held forwards, right hand holding rope hanging down behind, away you go.

A third method employs a wide webbed sling, laid across the buttocks in triangle shape, one corner dangling down between the legs; this corner is pulled through the legs, and joined by Karabiner to the other two corners coming round each side of the waist. Stand astride the abseil rope, lift it, clip it into the Karabiner, and screw down, the gate pointing away from you. With rope over left shoulder, held by left hand in front, and the descending rope held by the right hand behind you, away you go.

Various gadgets, such as descendeurs, etc, are available to help with an abseil, but a beginner should learn to abseil without them. For the times you are likely to need abseil (which is different from how many times you want to do it) the expense may not be justified.

Never let rumpled clothing be caught up in the abseil Karabiner, for hanging over a precipice in mid-air is not a good place to sort out a choked krab. The wise man wears leather gloves for abseiling, and stuffs some sort of pad on to his left shoulder to ease the tight bite of the rope. If, during abseiling, you find the rope is burning your flesh, grit your teeth and tell yourself it cannot last much longer. There is simply nothing else you can do.

The most difficult part of any abseil is going backwards over the edge, so do it quietly and deliberately, and know when you get over that it is all plain abseiling afterwards. The man who runs down with wild jumps is a fool, for nobody knows when an anchorage may give way. This sort of descent in fact places double the pull and friction on the anchorage, don't!

To protect the last man down an abseil, the one to go before can clip in a few running belays (stoppers) to prevent any slip. Another device used to slow down descent on an abseil rope is the Prussik knot, which can join your waist band to the abseil rope; if kept loose the knot slides down nicely, but if there is sudden hard pressure, it jams tight.

8 Other Equipment

Pitons and other Pegs

A piton is a metal peg for inserting into some crack in the rock to create an artificial hold for the ropes with which you work. There are two makes of piton, and these are used for different occasions:

Hard steel pitons do not bend. They create a powerful wedge.
Soft steel pitons bend as they are hammered into the crack, for they follow the lines of the crack. Often they must be abandoned, because they are difficult to extract and often unusable if recovered. They provide less security than hard steel pitons, so that it is important for them only to be used where the natural rock strengthens resistance to the turning moment of the tangential power of the eye in relation to the blade. (It is the eye through which a rope or Karabiner is placed.)

The Americans instituted high-tensile steel-alloy pitons, which have far better holding power than those made in Austria or Switzerland.

Types of Piton

The thickness and length of pitons varies according to the uses they are to be put to. Thickness also varies for cracks of different width. The simple blade or leaf piton is on sale in about three different sizes; the U-shaped or channel pitons grip strongly and are favoured for wide cracks; the V-shaped (angle or universal) type jams well in tight places; and the Leeper (or Z-shaped) piton, which also has strength and jams strongly, gives a good torque in both horizontal and vertical cracks.

The angle between the blade and the head (eye) of the piton is important in relation to the torque, i.e the turning moment of the tangential force, so that in some positions a head more easily bends and

HOW PITONS MOVE

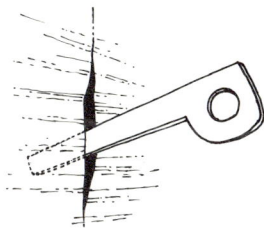

A.
VERTICAL, GOOD
CRACK NARROW ABOVE AND BELOW
NO TORQUE VALUE

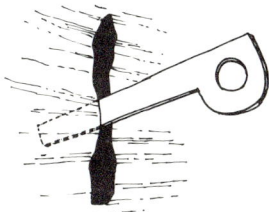

B.
VERTICAL, BAD
CRACK WIDE ABOVE AND BELOW
INSECURE – NO TORQUE VALUE

C.
SLANT, FAIR
REASONABLE TORQUE
SECURE

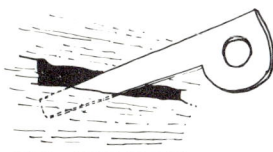

D.
HORIZONTAL, GOOD
TORQUE GOOD
SECURE

SHAPES OF PITON BLADES

RELATION OF
HEAD TO BLADE
'T' SECTION

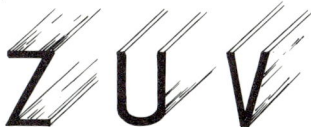

STRAIGHT   LEEPER   'U'   'V'
            (PROFILE)   (PROFILE)   (PROFILE)

OFFSET

91

snaps. If the piton has an offset relation head to blade or is of Leeper design, it will hold better in both horizontal and vertical cracks. Generally the larger the piton, the better its holding power, but this depends on the amount of its surface in touch with the rock into which it is hammered – one argument for the use of soft steel pitons.

Techniques

1 For a safe hold, about two-thirds of the piton should go into the crack without use of the hammer.

2 The piton hammer must have a wide head, for balancing on a rope with a toe perched on an inch of rock ledge is no place to fool around trying to hit a piton in. Generally the tail of the hammerhead ends in a good spike. The head must be fixed on with a metal sheath to the shaft so that it will not come off at some critical moment, and the end of the shaft should have a hole in the wood through which a loop of stout nylon cord can be looped.

3 You should not need more than three blows of the hammer to drive the piton into the crack, but always hammer the eye tight up to the rock.

4 While you hammer the piton in, listen to it, and if there is a high-pitched metallic sound, stop hammering. The crack will be a false one, with no secure hold. If there is a good bell-like chime to the metal, you can take it for granted that your piton is in a safe position, holding well. Should a dull, hollow, unmusical sound come from the hammering of the piton, it is not holding the rock properly. Do not trust it.

5 Do not hammer the piton any more once the eye is against the rock surface, for that can weaken it. Remember the piton must be able to go two-thirds of its length into the crack without hammering at all.

6 If the guidebook tells you that a rock climb requires twenty-five pitons, take twenty-seven with you, always two more than required. Do not rely on your friend Nobby's advice: 'I was there last week, and there are ten pitons still in place from last year.' Somebody could have removed those pitons an hour ago. Old pitons may have suffered corrosion, or metal fatigue. If you are re-using old pitons (we all do it), you must check carefully before a climb for cracks, especially at the place where the blade meets the eye.

7 Be careful that you do not place a piton at such an angle that you can neither thread rope or Karabiner through it.

8 Think before you place the piton in. How will the rope swing on it? A careless angle of swing between rope and piton could twist, weaken and even snap the head off the piton. Avoid pitons with eyes that do not allow easy movement of rope or Karabiner.

9 If you think the crack is not deep enough, use a short piton, which is much

safer than relying on a long piton not properly hammered home.

10 When you have returned to base, always clean mud and moisture from your pitons, and always keep them dry.

Uses of Pitons

A rock climber uses pitons, firstly, when going up the mountain; the piton then does not have to carry more than the weight of one climber at a time. In effect some liberty can be taken with the placing of the pitons for this manoeuvre.

The second use is for protection, especially on wholly artificial climbs (which cannot be made at all without pitons), for anchor on abseiling, and for main belays. In such cases it is safer to use two pitons at an angle. The pitons must be placed with great care, no risks being taken with the cracks, depth of pitons, or the type of piton used. They may have to take the force of a falling body. Lots of people suffer a slight slip without any damage at all, but the rope and piton placing must be good, strong and reliable.

Look at Your Cracks

No climber can always choose what sort of crack he hammers his pitons into, but the following information will help you decide when there is an option:

1 Horizontal cracks and cracks that slant give stronger holds than those running vertically.

2 Cracks that have the narrowest part at the bottom are safer than those that widen out at the bottom.

3 Never place a piton that is to be used for protection (main belay, abseil, etc) in a vertical crack.

4 Estimate the angle against which the pull on the rope could come, and then try to find a crack that is 90° to that pull.

5 The deeper and cleaner the crack, the better the hold. If a crack is shallow or filled with rubble, you cannot rely upon the sides to grip the piton sufficiently to provide a good hold.

HOW TO PLACE PITONS IN CRACKS

VERY GOOD

SATISFACTORY

CORRECT FOR PROTECTION OR PROGRESSION

DODGY

DANGEROUS

SUFFICIENT FOR PROGRESS — *NOT* FOR PROTECTION

HARD STEEL

SOFT STEEL

ENTRY OF PITONS

WRONG

1. BLIND CRACK
2. PITON UNSAFE

CORRECT

1. DEEP CRACK
2. PITON EYE VERY CLOSE TO ROCK

Getting the Piton Out

> This is the tale of Sunny Jim
> Who always left his pitons in
> But with his bank soon reached accord
> That he to climb could not afford.

It depends on how much climbing you do, how good the pitons are, and how badly damaged they are by previous use, but all climbers have to use and re-use pitons, because they are expensive. This means the last man on the rope takes out the pitons as he ascends, being well supported by the piton above himself.

Generally one uses the spike end of the hammerhead to prise pitons out. Strike the piton upwards and downwards along the line of the crack, back and forth, until it loosens. Sometimes one can attach a sling and jerk the peg out. Take your time when removing pitons. When the piton comes out, fix it to a shoulder loop or sling worn to carry pitons, etc.

Other Pegs

Hitherto the remarks have applied to pitons, partly because more care has to be taken with their placing, and partly because, if you can place a piton correctly and safely, the placing of other types of peg is relatively easy.

Many weird and wonderful aids are on the market. They may be classified as wedges, artificial chockstones and nuts. The object of the wedge is to jam in a gap too wide for pitons, and the aim of the latter two is to jam behind or in between anything that will hold them securely. These have a metal wire loop usually, through which the Karabiners or ropes can be passed. The use of aids such as screws and expanding bolts is frowned upon by all mountain users because these latter two aids tend to be by nature irremovable, and a permanent eyesore, if not source of damage, to the mountains.

Hollow wedges made of hard steel are called bongs. Never use an old wooden wedge. Where possible avoid wedges for use on main belay and abseil.

The weight exerted on a natural chockstone that is jammed in between two surfaces pulls the stone tighter in and makes the climber more secure. A sling is passed round the stone (usually attached

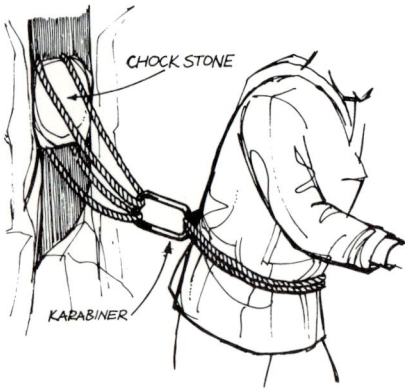

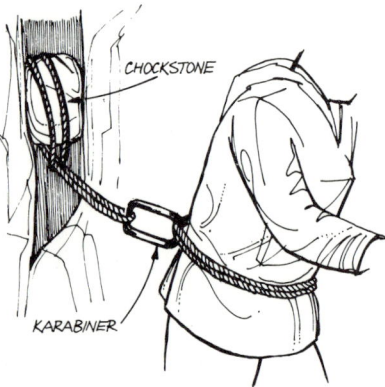

already to a steel artificial stone). Various nuts and other devices may be bought to act as artificial chockstones.

Karabiners

The rock climber necessarily carries an assortment of weighty objects with him, and Karabiners or Krabs are part of the load. His consolation is that he is rarely carrying them very far, and as his ascent continues, so his load lightens, unless he is the last man up, and has to carry them all back.

D-SHAPED KARABINER

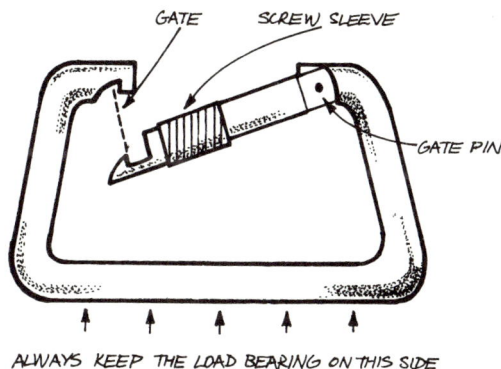

ALWAYS KEEP THE LOAD BEARING ON THIS SIDE

The Karabiner joins two ropes together, but prevents them fraying against one another. Modern climbers prefer Krabs to have a breaking strain of at least 4,000lb (1,814kg). They come in various shapes and sizes. The wise climber will stick to the simple D-shaped Karabiner (Figure 21). Never risk your life with a cheap unknown make that some guide or other recommended to you. A brand name has a guarantee of proper testing behind it. Unknown Krabs have failed disastrously – and a ghost cannot go back to the shop and complain! There is a gate on a spring that snaps shut to lock the rope in, but that is not enough. Over that gate, which is 6–7in (15–18cm) wide, comes a screw sleeve, which must at all times in use be screwed shut.

Do not judge a Krab by its weight, for that depends on the steel alloys used to make it. The mountaineering supplier will have the authenticated list of makers' products with the guaranteed breaking strain.

If at any time you are in doubt, use two Karabiners for main belay or waist ties. The art is to thread the moving rope through the Krab so that it cannot slip out if there is any sudden jar or strain on the gate side. A Krab used for attachment to the waist rope should have the gate facing downwards.

Be careful when fixing three Karabiners together that the movement of the rope (abseil, main belay, etc) will not twist one Krab against the other and force the gate to open (less likely if properly screwed shut). Most accidents occur because the climber was in too much of a hurry to screw the Krab up properly, and the breaking strain of an open Krab is often half that of a correctly closed one.

Avoid letting the gate crush against jagged rock under heavy pressure, in case the gate gives. Do not clip a Krab on to a piton in such a way that pressure forces the gate against the piton. If in doubt, use sling on piton, and Krab from sling to rope. Always check Krabs for metal fatigue, hairline cracks, etc. Never use old Krabs. Lastly, it cannot be said too often – take time, screw the gate shut properly. For further information on the uses of Karabiners, see Rope Techniques, p 73.

Etriers

These are a cross between a ladder and stirrups, and generally made of tough artificial fibres, of which plaited terylene is very good, especially if there is a wire inside the rope. Some are made with metal (aluminium alloy) steps, whereas others are just simple wide loops through which it is possible to push even a knee to keep balance. The depth of the tread varies, but 18in (45cm) apart is a good average.

Etriers are used for stiff rock climbs, where there are practically no reliable holds, but the rock allows for pitons to be placed in, through which one Karabiner is attached to another holding the etrier (make sure the gates of the Krabs do not become twisted by each other). Etriers are also used for steep ice in much the same way, and also for rescue from a crevasse.

Etriers are a most essential part of artificial climbing, in that they enable ascents to be made where no other way is feasible. It is much safer to have proper etriers than to make temporary ones from knotted slings.

While standing on an etrier, the climber (leader) is in an exposed position on what is virtually hostile rock, with no proper balance holds. The technique is made safer by having a second man haul on a rope (by leaning bodily against it) going through a Krab on a piton to the waist rope on the leader. This lessens damage in the case of a slip. The first move or two at the foot of the rockface are most likely reasonable, and from these the leader inserts his piton as high as is within controllable reach. He passes the rope through a Krab to his waist loop Krab, then attaches the etrier Krab, climbs easily, balances on the top and penultimate step (loop) and finds a good position for the next piton, and so on. It is easier in practice than the telling of it sounds.

ETRIER IN USE

A second etrier is commonly attached to the sling on which Krabs, pitons etc are loaded for transport.

A good rock climber can use etriers as a method of rest, sitting with legs through the loops as comfortably as if awaiting a cup of tea.

9 Winter Climbing

Climbing in snow and ice reveals some rare beauty. It is great sport, exciting and adventurous, and with a little care it can be kept like that. The following notes apply also to Alpine conditions; in fact you should never go to Switzerland or similar regions to climb (even in summer) if you have not had two or three long winter climbing holidays at home behind you.

Winter in mountain regions is as the weather says it is, with little relation to what a calendar in the valley below says. In winter you should reckon on daylight being four hours shorter and darkness four hours longer than during summer, which considerably affects (or should do) your planning of an ascent and return.

There is a sudden intensification of cold, and what was a comfortably warm day at 800ft (244m) in the valley becomes a subarctic terror at 4,000ft (1,219m), where the full force of the winter winds helps you understand what *Wuthering Heights* is all about. What is an enjoyable scramble in summer sunshine may turn out to be a very difficult or a severe climb in winter conditions.

For a start visibility is constantly being interrupted by cloud, mist, rain, sleet or snow. Nevertheless, men and women deliberately go out in these conditions, climb and return safely. The number of climbing accidents is nowhere near as great as accidents on a busy road during the rush-hour, and a climber is trained and alert to possible perils.

It is essential in winter to have one really experienced man in the party (if not more) who will check with all members that they know how to brake with an ice axe, use it as a balance aid in ascent, and know how to cut steps in the slopes. (There should be one ice axe per member.) Before you set out, make sure it is fully agreed that the leader's word is final. If he has to say 'Turn back', there must be no argument. His experience and knowledge have foreseen possibilities,

conditions, weather changes and so on that make it imperative to return.

Winter climbing has the same regular rhythmic movement to it as summer climbing, but you must double the emergency margin for complete expeditions. If you allow three hours ascent, three for descent, plus one hour emergency cover in summer, you must allow two hours for emergency cover in winter. Clearly this extra hour cannot be taken with any safety at the end of the day, when it is getting dark, so it means an early start. Here is your chance to welcome the dawn. It is easier to tackle lower slopes on the way up in light that is getting brighter all the time than to slither slowly and miserably back helping an injured friend when it is getting darker by the minute.

Winter climbing demands strict self and group discipline. If one person is not ready to start on time, you leave him behind. The schedule must be adhered to ruthlessly if you want to get your party back safely.

I have been on a mountain when, without warning, rain clouds made nightfall a couple of hours earlier than it should have been; if we had not been slightly ahead of schedule, we would have been trapped in an awkward place. In winter climbing, if the party feel fit (and I mean all of them), cut down rests at the summit, etc, if it means keeping on schedule or gaining a bit of time. Descents in winter can often take more care, which means more time, than ascents.

Sunshine on the mountains in winter is beautiful, improving the view and extending your panorama wonderfully, but it often deceives you about the low temperature prevailing. That may produce verglas, which is almost invisible ice and extremely slippery, on wet rock. A cold wind also can transform moisture on rocks into verglas quite quickly, though there may be no white snow nearby to indicate its presence.

Hillwalkers out for a winter ascent must keep off pure ice slopes, because an ice axe is of little use on them. But they can try slopes up to 30° quite safely. Those from 30° to 45° are steep, and those above that degree of incline are very slippery and hard, and only for very experienced rock climbers.

To go for a winter climb you should either have crampons ready to

Traversing a glacier

UPRIGHT TO CLIMB SNOW

LEAN INWARDS —
DOWN YOU GO!

UPRIGHT TO DESCEND

LEAN BACK —
DOWN YOU GO!

put on or specially nailed boots. Do not venture into snow and ice with only Vibrams or similar deeply indented rubber soles, for the indentations clog up quickly and the boots have no more resistance than waxed skis.

Ascent

Generally on slopes up to 30° you can go straight up easily and directly, using the ice axe spike to dig into the snow surface to give you a balancing hold. One climber should follow another, preferably using the same hole for his ice axe as the man before him.

On slopes above 30° in winter you would normally zigzag up, because this lessens the chance of one man's slip causing collision, chaos or catastrophe to the others (whether roped or not, and on such inclines in winter it is often advised by the leader that the party be roped (see p 73). Never lean forward into the mountain.

You hold your ice axe always in the hand that is highest up the hill, and when you zigzag, you change hands. In this way the ice axe is at once ready for use as a brake if need be, and not just as a balance hold.

Descent

Keep the weight on the heels. Remain upright, for leaning backwards leads to loss of balance. When you come to a steep pitch, face inwards to the slope, where you will feel safer. You will also have a better chance to control your movements, and be able to brake, if need be, with the ice axe.

Crampons

These give you securer holds over some rock, especially in snow and icy winter conditions. By giving you a grip, crampons also enable you to move with greater speed, although you must learn to make small steps, with the feet spaced well apart, clear of each other, when walking along the mountain in crampons. The unknown advantage of using crampons is that they keep the feet (boots) a fraction higher off of the ice and snow, and by this lessen the loss of heat. This may seem a minimal advantage, but over a length of time the cumulative effect is noticeable. The use of crampons also avoids the need to cut steps one at a time in ice slopes, which is in itself a great time-saver.

CRAMPONS

ONE STRAP ONLY IS SHOWN

NOTE HOW THEY ARE STRAPPED TO BOOT

When buying crampons, there are a number of points to remember:

1 It is cheaper to buy a good pair. Avoid those with less than ten claw points on them, for ten are needed to give you a fairly steady hold. The claws are usually $1\frac{1}{4}$in (32mm) long, but sometimes shorter claws are used if the climb is not just on iced rock, but on solid ice slopes also.
2 Lobsters are crampons with two spikes in front (making twelve on each

crampon), and these spikes slope diagonally forwards and downwards. They enable the climber to kick into the ice and hold better on very steep places, and are useful if you encounter ice slopes with an additional covering of snow.

3 Crampons slow down normal pace, but speed up your movements over ice and snow. They can easily become clogged with wet snow, and must be tapped free with the shaft of your ice axe, which you would naturally carry in conditions when crampons would be required.

4 Be careful how you walk when wearing crampons over your boots, for they can tear socks, clothing and flesh badly. When you first buy them, spend some time learning how to move delicately in them. You should be a good climber with experience of winter climbing on less severe slopes, and thus have acquired a good sense of balance and mountain sense, before you need crampons. If you should fall while wearing crampons, they could cause terrible injuries; they also make the faller tend to somersault.

5 Only buy crampons with quick-release bindings. The fastenings must be on the outside of the foot.

6 Crampons must fit the boots tightly, not only to avoid slipping, but because loose crampons could have a disastrous psychological effect on you. So when you buy crampons, take your climbing boots along, fit them on, and then shake the boot slowly and hard. If the crampons slip, they are too loose.

7 When you carry crampons, keep them strapped to the rucksack, points inwards to the sack. Some climbers use a block of wood or polystyrene over the claws.

8 Always dry crampons after use. Check them for hairline cracks. Dropping them from a great height can damage them. File the points to keep them sharp. Always check sharpness of points, and security of fastenings before you begin your ascent.

9 If the ice slope is steep, dig the toe of the crampon deep down into the ice; always use small steps and keep feet wide apart.

10 If the ice is not unduly steep, you do not need to kick so deeply into the ice, but strengthen your balance by use of the ice axe.

11 It will be easier to zigzag up a slope to relieve the strain on the ankles that wearing crampons usually produces, especially the first time.

12 Lobsters make a direct ascent easier than other crampons, but are not always advisable.

Ice Axe

As climbers ruefully admit, there is no such thing as an ideal ice axe; it is always a question of compromise. If there is a long climb with much rock predominant, you only need a light ice axe, but for a long ice climb you will need a heavy axe. A long axe is better for belaying, but a shorter axe for cutting steps in the ice. The steeper the ice slope encountered, the shorter the ice axe should be – generally about 20in (50cm). The average length of a general purpose ice axe is about 30in (76cm). The end of the shaft has a spike, and as a rough guide this should be longer by a middle finger joint than the height of your climbing boot-toe. Early climbers thought nothing of carrying a 3ft (91cm) ice axe up with them. The wise climber carries a tight-fitting rubber stopper to clamp on the spike when not in use. There is a tendency for the old hickory shafts to be replaced by alloys such as hiduminium, etc. The pros and cons are debatable rather than proven fact, but it seems that the alloys are probably stronger for belays by ice axe than the wood.

The ice axe must be carried with the spike pointing forwards and down, the head tucked underneath your arm. If not wanted for the moment, it is carried on the climber's sack, which will have special straps to hold it in position, the spike usually pointing upwards.

Most ice axes have a wrist loop, for holding on to in emergency. Remember that if you lose the ice axe because of a slip, you may be in real trouble, but if you fall and hold on to the axe, you have the chance of braking (see below), which may save you further injury from rocks and boulders. Therefore, hold on to your ice axe if you slip.

How to Brake

The thick end of the metal head is called the adze. The thin end is the pick, the under side of which should have a good saw edge. If you slip, grip the adze tight into your right shoulder (unless you are left-handed, when it would be left shoulder) right hand uppermost, left hand gripping pick end of the head, and force the pick with all your weight into the snow slope. Keep the spike lifted well back behind you to increase the depth of the pick's bite into the snow. If you are wearing crampons, lift your feet back behind you, or they might make you somersault backwards. Ordinary nailed boots tend to slow down your progressive slip when you dig the soles against the snow.

You will notice I said snow, although this implement is called an ice axe. Its best braking power is in fact on snow, for really deep ice is often too tough to allow the axe to be fully effective. But try it all the same if need be.

To practise braking, go to an easy snow-covered slope about 25ft (7·6m) high, with a gentle angle, and a good layer of snow on the slope and at the bottom. Then, unencumbered by any other equipment than the axe, let yourself slip. Under the conditions in which you would normally be carrying an ice axe you would also be wearing mitts or gloves. The more practice you get, the safer you will be, for the movement becomes quite instinctive after a few goes.

Even hillwalkers should carry an ice axe if they go out in winter. In mixed climbing terrain the leader had best carry a short axe, and the second man a longer axe, to cover all eventualities. Other members should also carry longer axes, because they are more useful for belays.

ICE AXE BELAY

It is winter and the snow is thick upon the ground – much winter climbing is done in wide gullies – so that there is not any obvious secure belay. You come to a tricky part where the fall by one of the roped party might lead to a fall by all – so the answer is to belay.

Use your boots to kick in a fair-sized step in the hard snow. Push the ice axe straight down up to its head in the snow, tie a figure eight knot in the rope, stand down a little lower, and place the belay over the head of the axe; it is tightened for the knot, and runs slightly down to where you have linked it to your waist rope, and then on downwards to the next climber.

Another way is for the first man to put the axe in as described above, but to put his foot upon the head, and pass the rope round himself. This is sometimes better if the snow is not very hard.

CUTTING STEPS

It is better to do this with the boots than with an axe, provided the slope is soft enough (see Crampons, p 105). However, if you must use the axe for cutting steps (on a slope of 40° or more), try to cut through to the ice, not just in the snow alone. Use both hands to cut with, and do not waste energy or lose too much time. Swing the axe so that the head bites into the ice. Make the first step broad enough and deep enough to stand upon easily. The next need be only a small balance hold, followed by a broad deep step, and then by a toe-hold, alternating all the way up. When you are on a good broad deep step, cut the next two up.

Think where you are going before you cut, for diagonally may be easier than straight up. On very tough ice cut the step horizontally, so that your foot stands sideways, rather than into the mountain; this can save time.

You cut with the adze, reserving the pick for very tough ice, or where a large step is needed for a rest. Steps should incline downwards; they need not be flat. This gives better hold and balance.

Ice Hammers, Pitons and Screws

Hammers are generally required only for winter climbs where snow and ice are certain, or in expensive Alpine expeditions. The ice hammer resembles an ordinary piton hammer, except that its pick is much longer, which is better for cutting large steps in steep ice slopes, and makes it much easier to extract ice pitons.

Ice pitons are made of harder steel than is necessary for ordinary pitons. It is important to keep the line of maximum anticipated drag by the rope at 90° angle to the widest part of the ice piton. Some Continental types are made with rings attached to the pitons, but these are

dangerous in any climbing, particularly in ice and snow. You need an ice piton to which a Karabiner can be attached, which is much safer (see Karabiners, p 96).

Ice screws have the advantage of not splitting the ice open or into flakes as easily as do ordinary ice pitons. Some people maintain that it is easier to unscrew an ice screw than lever out a piton.

A flat, metal 'dead-man' with a wire sling makes a good belay in snow and ice.

Winter/Alpine Climbs at High Altitude

1 Lack of oxygen slows down and blurs the mental processes. The higher you climb, the rarer the oxygen content of the atmosphere becomes. It depends upon the climber, experience, physical condition, etc, as to the altitude at which breathing becomes more difficult. Some notice it painfully at 10,000ft (3,049m), others are quite happy up to 18,000ft (5,486m). This is one of the dangers that tourist propaganda ignores when it seeks to lure young, relatively inexperienced climbers to the Swiss Alps, and other high mountains.

2 Deterioration. Sir John Hunt first reported the speed with which muscle tissues deteriorate around 25,000ft (7,620m) and above, and the climber soon notices subsequent to this a reduced resistance to the intense cold, and a reduced capacity to withstand the wind.

Negotiating an ice overhang

10 First Aid and Serious Emergencies

First Aid

ANKLES

See Sprains, Twisted Ankles, p 118.

BURNS AND SCALDS

These come from an accident with cooking equipment while bivouacking, etc. Apply a dry sterile dressing to the wound. If clothing sticks to a dry burn, leave it on. If clothing adheres to a scald, lift the textile away.

CRAMP

Rest, apply warmth to affected muscles. I usually carry some salt and eat a pinch of it if I think cramp is coming on.

CUTS, WOUNDS AND BLEEDING

The most important thing is to stop the bleeding. Remove clothing to check whether the bleeding is dangerous or not. Apply a clean dressing, then apply firm pressure by a pad on top of it. Bandage up the wound. Morphia lessens bleeding and takes away the pain of a serious wound, but never give morphia if there is an injury to the head or if the patient is already unconscious. It is inadvisable to give stimulants where there is serious bleeding. Wipe out obvious impurities, such as moss or grit, and apply liquid or powder antiseptic to cuts and wounds. Then apply dressing, elastoplast, cotton-wool, etc.

TOURNIQUET

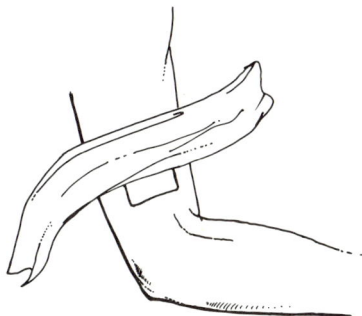

PAD OVER WOUND

BANDAGE SLIGHTLY ABOVE WOUND

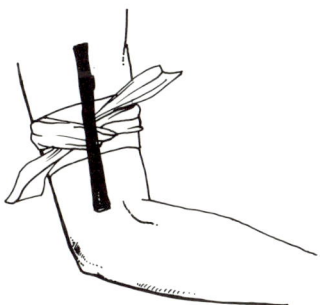

FIRST KNOT: COMPRESSION STICK READY

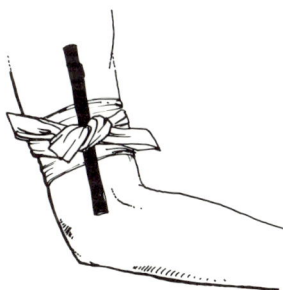

STICK TWISTED AFTER BEING
SECURED IN FIRST KNOT

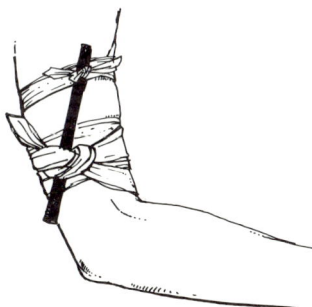

HIGHER KNOT TO HOLD
STICK IN PLACE

TEN MINUTE NOTE
THIS TOURNIQUET APPLIED FIRST AT 16⁰⁰ 10 MINS SHIFT

(Generally it is unwise to plug a deep wound, because this could force germ-carrying agents deeper in.)

If there is severe arterial bleeding this must be dealt with at once by a tourniquet. Press a smooth thick pad of clean cloth or a bandage on the wound, and keep in place by a turn of bandage. Above the wound apply a broad clean bandage under the injured limb only once; do not be heavy-handed or forceful in fastening this, and try hard not to jerk the injured limb or drag it while trying to help the patient.

The knot and compression stick of the tourniquet are placed above the wound, to the heart side of the patient's body. The stick is twisted until the pulse below the tourniquet can no longer be felt. Then fix the stick in that position with a second knot above the first. If possible, make a note of the exact time the tourniquet was applied. At ten-minute intervals (at the most fifteen minutes) you must release the tourniquet. At first there may be slight bleeding, but this will stop after two or three applications of the tourniquet. The blood contains natural coagulant properties which, given help by the tourniquet, will prevent further loss of blood. Serious damage can be done if the tourniquet is not loosened every ten minutes.

EXPOSURE

This is the accumulated effect of cold (wind), dampness (mist equally as well as rain), and tiredness. It is not easily recognised the first time you encounter it. The symptoms are (1) increased irritability, (2) feelings of cold, cramp and of tiredness, (3) mental and physical lethargy, (4) slurred speech and failure to understand what is said, and (5) some abnormality of vision. If these symptoms are not attended to at once, collapse and coma may ensue.

For treatment stop at once at the nearest convenient place, for further exertion may lead to the collapse, or even death of the patient. Insulate him against further loss of heat, using the space blanket or the polythene sheet. If you cannot find shelter, build a bivouac or tent; this is essential if the weather turns really nasty. The first thing to do is to place sufficient insulating material between the patient and the cold ground, remembering that the ground is always cold. If there is no other warmth available, lie close to the patient and warm him with your own body heat. Give him glucose, sugar or condensed milk. Keep cheerful, and do not let the patient give way to despair. Do not massage the patient to improve his circulation, and do not give him alcohol.

FRACTURES

Immobilise a fracture to prevent broken bones causing internal damage, or bursting through the skin (which allows access of bacteria to the tissues so torn.) The immobilisation must take place before the patient is placed on a stretcher. Do not try straightening a broken limb.

Arm. Bandage the upper arm to the chest. If it is possible to use some part of your equipment as a splint, apply this to the arm before bandaging the forearm to the chest or in a sling.

Collarbone. Put hand of the damaged side up to the opposite (whole) collarbone, then bandage the entire arm and shoulder to the chest.

Jaw. Little can be done before help arrives, but do not let the patient lie on his back, or he could choke.

Leg. Bandage the damaged limb to the sound limb. Put pads between the knees and the ankles. Bandage at the hips, knees and ankle. Use as splint if available. Never try to straighten a broken leg, and do not move it.

Neck. Treat with great care and delicacy. Put the patient gently on his back. Use a pair of boots to keep the head still, placing one boot on either side, uppers under the nape of the neck. If you have a triangular bandage, fasten the boots to the head with ties across the forehead and the chin.

Spine. This is difficult to be sure about. If in any doubt, avoid moving the patient. You can do nothing except keep him warm and talk as cheerfully as possible until a rescue team and stretcher arrive. Signs of spinal damage are numbness in the legs and general ill-defined pains in the back.

Generally commonsense and experience should warn you not to venture on a climb where serious injuries become more likely in view of the terrain, weather, lack of experience, without having sufficient climbers in the party to handle serious emergencies. Two is inadequate; three or four a safer proposition.

FROSTBITE

Apply the warmth of another body or breathe heavily on the part to be warmed. There are conflicting views about rubbing the part with snow, which is a traditional method of dealing with the condition. Do not massage frostbite with your hands. Do not bang or knock frost-bitten parts – if the frostbite is very severe, the part might chip off. Frostbite is something that should never happen to a climber, but the experienced are often more careless than the inexperienced.

HEAD INJURY

If climbers are wearing the recommended safety helmets, head injuries should be rarely met with, but there is often some child or fool kicking stones over the edge. I was in a chimney once when there was a sudden fall of stones, cause unknown; if I had not been wearing my helmet, I might not be writing this book now. In cases of bleeding use a sterile pad and bandage, applying them firmly. Check that the patient's mouth, nose and throat are free of obstructions (use a finger to do this if the patient cannot tell you).

HEAT EXHAUSTION

If a climb is made in summer or during hot dry weather, climbers, especially those carrying heavy loads, can suffer from this condition. Beginners do not realise how very dehydrating and oppressive the reflected heat from sheer rock can be. Move the patient to the coolest shelter available, or at least keep your own body between the patient and the sun. Loosen his clothing, use anything as a fan, keep him calm and still. When climbing with Kurt Müller I got used to carrying tomatoes instead of water, but later from Ryuzo Nakamura I acquired the habit of taking lemons to suck; they are sour but very thirst-quenching.

SHOCK

This condition frequently accompanies all sorts of mountain accidents. It is essential to recognise the symptoms. The patient usually goes very pale, and feels very much like fainting but rarely does so. His pulse beats very fast but seems to be weaker in the violence of its throb. The skin goes cold and becomes moister than normal. The patient usually begins to gasp for air, the breathing becoming shallow and often quicker. Do not let the patient's body contact the ground, for there is always a cold quality about mountain rock. Do not over-heat the patient (no need for space blankets here). Talk cheerfully to him, for he is feeling much more ill than looks indicate. There is often concomitant injury, so deal with this as soon as possible. Do not give alcohol if you suspect internal injuries. Make the patient lie down (insulated from the rocks), feet slightly higher than the head.

Secondary shock may start within an hour of the accident. This is often pronounced when the patient showed little or no sign of primary shock at the time of the accident. Keep the patient recumbent (as above), comfortable, and warm but not overheated. Always stop bleeding before any other treatment. If there is no abdominal injury or other serious apparent damage internally, give him a warm drink if it is available, with a little salt and sugar added. The patient must have plenty of oxygen.

SNAKES

The lower slopes of mountains, and some mountains in the southern hot areas of the temperate zone and tropics, have the additional hazard of snakes. Very few snake bites are lethal, so keep calm and keep the patient quiet. Examine the bite carefully. A poisonous bite shows two distinct punctures and only one row of serrate (tooth)

SNAKE BITES

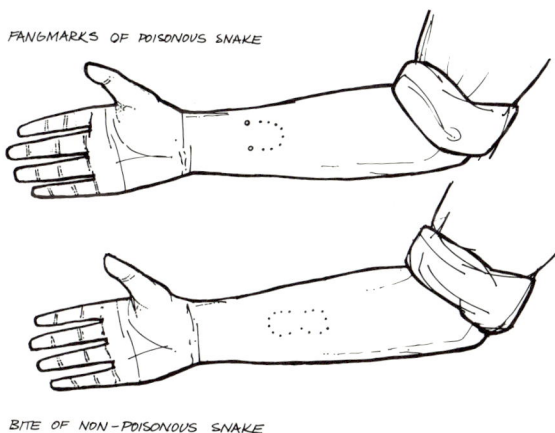

FANGMARKS OF POISONOUS SNAKE

BITE OF NON-POISONOUS SNAKE

marks, by which hold the snake levers its poisonous fangs into the flesh. Apply a tourniquet see (p 113) between the point of the wound and the heart.

Use alcohol, lemon juice, garlic or onion juice to sterilise the skin.

Use a flame to sterilise a knife or razor blade (a match or two if nothing else), and make an X-shaped cut in two strokes, each slit about ½in long and about ⅛in deep over each fang point. Try to avoid arteries and veins. Suck hard and spit the issuing blood and poison out in a steady rhythmic process (the rhythm makes it easier for the helper). This may take a long time – as much as half an hour. If there is a swelling after this time suck for ten minutes out of every thirty until help arrives. In snake bite alcohol is often of more use to the rescuer than to the rescued, although it has some antiseptic properties and can be used to clean the wound.

Always get the patient to a doctor, even if the poison seems wholly cleared up. Always assume, unless you are an expert herpetologist, that every snake bite you cannot identify is poisonous, just in case. Never give morphia for snake bite.

SPRAINS, TWISTED ANKLES

These are a preliminary form of dislocation, with damage to the ligament and muscles at the joint. It is always more painful than it looks. The patient needs rest from movement at the earliest possible moment, and until then a splint made from any equipment available can be used to limit (prevent, if feasible) movement and also protect the joint from knocks and shocks.

There is usually considerable internal bleeding at the place of the sprain, and this brings with it a swelling and tenderness. A bandage soaked in cold water or snow reduces the bleeding; it should be applied firmly but not tightly. Try to avoid allowing a sprained joint to hang downwards. When you reach the valleys, take the patient to a doctor, and have the joint X-rayed.

With twisted ankles, unlace but do not remove the boot unless it is certain there is no fracture (degree of pain and angle of twisted joint are ready guides to that). If salt is available, put some round the ankle when dressing the sprain with a bandage. Bandage the ankle firmly to

A vision of beauty and danger

limit the extent of swelling. The injured person may be able to hobble along with another person providing a shoulder for him to balance on. If he cannot, a stick or crutch needs be improvised.

Rescue Work

Always inform somebody where you are going, which route you are following, and when you expect to be back. Then advise them when you have returned. If travelling to the climb by car, leave the details just specified on the car windscreen. Check where the nearest rescue post is before you set out.

Take light and sound (whistle) equipment for signalling with you, making certain they work. Take spare bulb and new batteries. Internationally the signals of distress for mountains are as follows:

> six long blasts on the whistle at one-minute intervals
> six long flashes of a torch at night

The answer ('I have seen your signal') is

> three long blasts or flashes

Serious Emergencies

Emergencies happen when they are least expected, testing our ability to react to them. Once they have been survived, they often prove to have been strengthening beneficial events, turning points for greater progress and success than we could have foreseen at the time. Knowledge is the best safeguard against emergencies, and beyond that the keynotes are imagination and improvisation. Remember that the quickest way out of an emergency is to deal with it safely, slowly and surely. As soon as the emergency becomes evident, pause, take ten deep breaths, examine the situation, and start to see how best to deal with it. Here are some ideas that will help you deal with some difficult situations.

SNOWED-UP

1 To go on may well be suicidal. Find a deep drift on the safest ledge or area available.
2 Cut out a snow hole with your ice axe. Use your hands only in the last

A SNOW HOLE

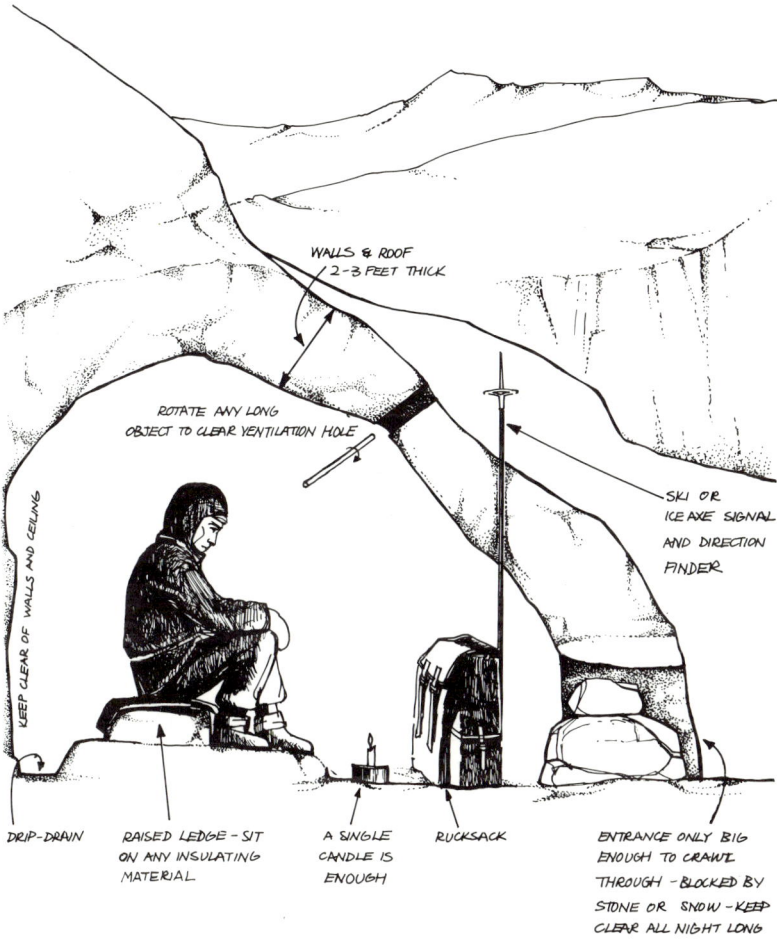

WALLS & ROOF
2-3 FEET THICK

ROTATE ANY LONG
OBJECT TO CLEAR VENTILATION HOLE

KEEP CLEAR OF WALLS AND CEILING

SKI OR
ICE AXE SIGNAL
AND DIRECTION
FINDER

DRIP-DRAIN

RAISED LEDGE – SIT
ON ANY INSULATING
MATERIAL

A SINGLE
CANDLE IS
ENOUGH

RUCKSACK

ENTRANCE ONLY BIG
ENOUGH TO CRAWL
THROUGH – BLOCKED BY
STONE OR SNOW – KEEP
CLEAR ALL NIGHT LONG

resort and if the snow is really soft, or the cold on your hands may lower body temperature and induce exposure.

3 Remove a pullover, sweater and any nylon garments before beginning the dig, because it is unlikely that the muscles will chill while in movement (unlike bare hands on snow), and the amount of cold felt will not harm you as much as sweating. Perspiration is wet and this moisture can freeze and kill you.

4 The entry to the snow hole should be only big enough for a man to crawl through. Once inside, you scoop out more snow to enlarge the hole internally, passing the snow outside to a friend, who shovels it away.

5 You tunnel upwards, creating a hemisphere dome, because this has, architecturally, a powerful structural resistance.

6 The digging of a hole large enough for two may take two hours, depending upon the texture of the snow.

7 Make a hole for ventilation in addition to the entry hole. This must be kept free from further snowfall during the night, so an ice-axe shaft or similar pole must be used to poke up the ventilation hole at frequent intervals to keep it free. The entry hole should also be kept free of snowfall. In the Arctic we commonly put some object near the sleeping bag, so that when you wake up, you can see which way is up. The reason is that people can feel panic and disorientation if awakening in a snow hole, especially for the first time.

8 When inside the hole, stamp and punch all surfaces to make the area really smooth; this gives you added protection. Make a drip-drain all round the cave on the internal perimeter, and run it out of the main entry.

9 Build a platform of snow up from the surface (easily done as you create the drip-drain). This is to elevate the sleeping bags etc. Use anything available to insulate the body from the snow surface, and from the ice walls and roof. And insulate as much as possible. This hole will be extremely warm and comfortable if you do things right.

10 Keep light and heating down to one candlepower, unless the hole is big enough to stand two without producing condensation. Experience will show you quickly. It is possible to warm liquids and cook in such a hole, and to sleep well, but in shifts; one of the party must be on watch all night long to keep the snow-hole entry and ventilation clear, even if it has temporarily stopped snowing. A watch can be two, three or four hours long. Short watches mean interrupted sleep, but make it more likely that the guard stays awake.

I would like to record my thanks to Bjorn Bått of Mosjøn, Norway, who first taught me these techniques nearly thirty years ago.

A BOULDER BIVOUAC

BOULDER 'D' ADDED TO 'C' TO FILL GAP

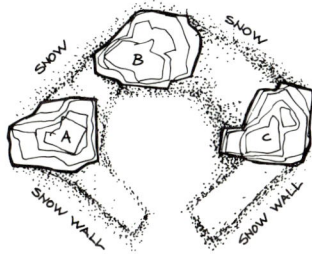

A

B

D

C

SNOW

SNOW

SNOW

B

A

C

SNOW WALL

SNOW WALL

SNOW BRICKS

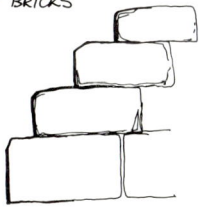

ICE AXE MAKES VENTILATOR HOLE

USE RUCKSACK FRAMES, SKIS ETC, TO HELP MAKE A ROOF

BOULDER BIVOUAC

If there is no snow ledge, or conditions do not allow for the digging of a nice warm snow hole, find a spot where some boulders are obligingly near one another. Use stones and snow to build walls between the existing boulders as required. The main object is to cut off the wind and snow or sleet. Snow will be warmer than the rock, so pad the inside with snow bricks. I reckon on a 2ft 6in (76cm) thickness of walls. Your rucksack frames and anything else around can be used to roof the area in. Do not try to make a snow-brick roof unless you are building a perfectly circular igloo, which requires a lot of practice and a good knife to cut the snow into regularly sized bricks. The boulder bivouac is nowhere near as good a shelter as a snow hole.

GENERAL NOTES

1 If you need water to cook or just to drink, melt ice not snow. Ice melts more quickly and gives more water.
2 If the matches are wet, rub them very slowly in your hair, which should dry them. I usually carry some in a waterproof container.
3 Remember that, if you have no other means of signalling, the lid of a food tin can be rubbed bright and used to flash sunlight. This method was used by the Apaches originally; they employed any bright metal object to signal from hilltop to hilltop.
4 If you are seriously stranded and need to make a fire, you can use a camera lens to light it. Remove the film, place the opened back of the camera towards the sun, and focus rays on any scraps of paper, cloth, etc, to start the fire.
5 You can only start a fire with very small scraps of dry material, and whatever you have to tear up, it is worth lighting.
6 If nothing else is to hand, use ice to make a lens. You need it 1in (2·54cm) thick, and you can use hand heat to smooth it round and domed on the one side, keeping the reverse flat and smooth. The ice should be as big as a man's hand. Balance the ice-lens between finger and thumb, turn the domed side to the sun, and place the inflammable material beneath the flat side. A friend's finger can soon tell which is the hottest spot. That is where you place the fire to be.
7 In case of lightning keep away from caves and wet rocks. Place ice axe and crampons, Karabiners, etc, well away from where you shelter. Bunch up small. Split the party up into twos – not more – and keep well apart.

Glossary of Welsh Names

Wales contains some of the best climbing in the world. Sir John Hunt, Hillary and the team that climbed Everest trained in Wales. Nobody who knows the Welsh mountains can fail to appreciate and love them. To help climbers understand the map names I include a glossary, dedicated to my friend Mrs Eluned Roberts of Tywyn, who gave me my first lessons in Welsh, and respectfully to the Merched y Wawr, who do so much to keep their beautiful language in everyday use.

> Drwy lwybrau gwyn yr evia awn
> Pob un a'i gân, pob un a'i ddawn;
> Rhydd pawb ei ran mewn sain a swyn . . .

> We trot along paths white with the snow
> Each with a song, each with his talent,
> Each gives all he can in sound and joy as we go . . .

Aber	Estuary, river mouth	*Betws*	Chapel
Adar, adeyn	Bird, birds	*Blaen, blaenau*	High point, head of
Adwy	Pass		a valley
Ael	Ridge, edge, brow	*Boch*	Cheek
Afon	River	*Bod*	Home, house
Allt	Wooded hillside	*Braich*	Arm, branch of a
Aran	High peak		hill, river
Arddu	Black crags	*Bran*	Crow
Bach (Fach)	Small	*Bras*	Fat
Bala	Lake	*Bron*	Slope of a hill
Ban	High point, peak,	*Bryn*	A hill
	crest, beacon	*Bryncyn*	A small hill
Barrug	Hoar frost	*Bwlch*	Gap, pass, col, notch
Bedd	Grave, burial place	*Bychan*	Small, tiny
Bedw, bedwen	Birch tree, trees	*Cadair (Gadair)*	Chair
Bera, bere	Hilltop, point	*Cae*	Field

Glossary of Welsh Names

Caer	Fort, camp	Chwarel	Quarry
Canol	Middle	Dau	Two
Capel	Large chapel	Derw, derwen	Oak (s)
Carn	Heap of stones	Dinas	A natural fortification
Carnedd, -au	Stony hill and plural,		point in Roman and
	also cairn and head		Saxon times
Carreg	Stone (plural, cerrig)	Dol	Meadow in a small
Castell	Castle		valley
Cau	Hollow place	Drosgl	Rough, boulder-clad
Cefn	Ridge, backbone		hill
Cegin	Kitchen	Drum	Exposed but usually
Celyn	Holly		smooth ridge
Cidwm	Wolf	Drws	Door
Cigfran	Raven	Du, ddu	Black
Cilfach	Nest, nook, niche	Dwr, dwfr	Water
	on the rocks	Dyffryn	Watered valley
Clip	Bluff	Dyn	Man
Clogwyn	Precipice	Dysgl	Dish, hollowed-out
Cludair	Pile, heap		place in the
Clwyd	Gate		mountains, like a
Clyd	Shelter		soup plate
Cnicht	Knight	Eglwys	Church
Coch (Goch)	Red	Eigion	Depths, bottom
Coed	Trees, woods	Eira, eiry	Snow
Collen (Gollen)	Hazel trees	Eryri	Eagle's nest, any
Congl	Corner, angle		high isolated point
Corn	Horn	Esgair	Side, usually a steep
Cors	Bog		ridge
Crach	Dwarf	Fach	Small
Craig	Rough rock	Faes	Meadow
Criafol	Rowan	Fan	Beacon (highest
Crib	Jagged ridge		point of a hill)
Cribin	Sawtoothed ridge of	Fawr (Mawr)	Large
	a hill	Foel (Moel)	Bald hill, no
Crochan	Pit, cauldron		vegetation
Croes	Cross	FF	Separate letter of
Cromlech	Massive monumental		Welsh alphabet
	stone erected by	Ffordd	Road
	ancient Britons	Ffynon	Spring or well
Crug	Mound, heap	Gallt	A small hill
Cwm	Valley	Ganol	Central
Cymer	Coming together, as	Garn	Eminence
	of streams, valleys,	Gawr	Raging torrent
	etc	Glas	Blue-green colour
CH	Separate letter of	Gluadair	Heaped stones
	Welsh alphabet	Glyn	Deep narrow valley
Chwa	Breeze	Goch	Red

Golau	Light	*Merch, merched*	Woman, women, daughter(s)
Golwg	View	*Mign*	Bog
Golygfa	Wide view over distance	*Min*	Edge, lip
Gors	Swamp	*Moel*	Bare hill, no vegetation
Grug	Heather	*Mor*	Sea
Gwalch	Hawk	*Mur*	Wall
Gweryd	Stretch of moss-covered ground	*Mynach*	Monk
Gwy	Water	*Mynydd*	Mountain
Gwyn, gwen	White	*Nant*	Valley, usually wide
Gwynt	Wind	*Newydd*	New
Hafod	Summer shieling for shepherds	*Oer*	Cold
		Ogof	Cave
Haul	Sun	*Onn*	Ash tree
Hebog	Hawk	*Pair*	Wide cauldron
Helgi	Hunting dog	*Pant*	Hollow valley
Helyg, helygen	Willow (s)	*Pen*	Head, top of a mountain
Hen	Old		
Hendref	Winter home, shelter	*Penmaen*	Rocky headland
Hir	Long	*Penrhyn*	Promontory
Hydd	Stag	*Pentref*	Village
Hyll	A place with an eerie feeling, gloomy, ugly	*Pentwr*	Pile or heap
		Pistyll	Waterfall, the spring of a river that starts as a spout
Isaf	Lowest		
LL	A separate letter of the Welsh alphabet	*Plas*	Big house
		Pont	Bridge
Llan	Church	*Porth*	Port
Llech	Flat stone	*Pwll*	Pool
Llefn	Smooth	*Rhaeadr, rhayader*	Waterfall
Llithrig	Slippery		
Lloer	Moon	*Rhigol*	Cleft, groove
Llugwy	Light appearing	*Rhiw*	Smooth hill slope
Llwybr	Path	*Rhos*	Upland moor
Llwyd	Grey	*Rhyd*	Ford
Llwyn	Grove	*Rhyferthwy*	Mountain torrent, river in spate
Llyn	Lake		
Llys	Court	*Saeth*	Arrow
Ma, man	Place	*Sarn*	Causeway
Maen	Solid block of stone	*Serth*	Precipitous
Maes	Field	*Syth, seth*	Straight
Main	Narrow	*Tal*	Head, end, lofty
Mawr	Large	*Talar*	Headland of a field or piece of land
Meirch	Horse		
Melin	Windmill	*Tan*	Under, below
Melyn, melen	Yellow		

Tref	Homestead, town, occasionally hamlet	*Yn*	In, in the, at the
Tri	Three	*Ynys*	An islet of solid land amid a bog
Troed	Foot	*Ysbyty*	Hospital
Troetffordd	Footpath	*Ysfa*	Sheepwalk
Trum	Ridge, exposed, usually smooth	*Ysgol, ysgollon*	Ladder(s)
		Ysgubor	Barn
Twll	Hole, cavern	*Ystrad*	Wide farmed valley, town street
Twmpath	Small hill		
Ty	House	*Ystum*	Curve or bend
Uchaf	Highest	*Ystwyth*	Winding, twisting
Un	One	*Ywennol*	Foaming
Y, yr	The		

All the above are to be found in place names. Note also *Llwybr cyhoeddus* – public footpath. 'Thank you' is *Diolch yn fawr* in Welsh. My friend Bernard Newman used to say nobody should visit a country without being able to say thank you in its language.

Entry in a club book: 'Ascended the Needles in five minutes, found them very easy'. Below someone wrote: 'Descended the Needles in five seconds, found them very hard'!

Glossary of Scottish Names

The mountains of Scotland are not only beautiful but addictive, offering variations that will satisfy and delight all grades of climbers. In some of the most exciting areas the ancient Gaelic tongue is in common daily use, and increasing in vitality and popularity thanks to the efforts of the Gaelic Speaking Society.

One of the attractions of Gaelic is that it provides a stimulating series of subtle changes in spelling according to rules that have been followed from time immemorial.

Ch has a powerful aspirated sound, somewhat stronger than in German *Nacht*

Fh is not pronounced generally

Mh, and *bh* are both pronounced as V

The definite article changes with the gender, number and case of the noun it introduces, and further modifications occur according to the initial letter of the noun it precedes: Am, an, an t', a', na, na h', nam, nan.

Abar, aber		*Aoineadh*	Steep headland
(*Obar*)	Mouth of a river	*Ban*	White, fair
Abhainn,		*Barp*	A large cairn with
amhuinn, avon	River		interior shelter
Ach, achadh	Field on upland	*Barr*	A conical top
	terrain	*Beag, beg*	Small
Ailean	Green place, a plain	*Bealach*	Gap, high pass
Airidh	Summer shieling	*Beinn, ben*	Mountain
Aisir	Narrow, rocky	*Beul*	Mouth
	defile, a pass	*Binnean, binnein*	A mount
Ald, alt, allt,		*Both, bothan*	Hut
ault	Mountain stream	*Brae, braigh,*	
Aird, ard	High point	*bread*	Summit

'Blue are the hills that are far away' (Gaelic proverb)

Bruaich	Steep place	*Ear*	East
Cadha	Steep pass	*Eas, easach*	Waterfall, cascade
Carn, cairn	Heap of stones to mark a path, point, etc	*Easg*	Bog
		Eilean	Island
		Fad, fhada	Long
Caol (Gaolas)	Narrow	*Feadan*	Canyon, narrow valley
Carr	Rough stony ground, covered with boulders	*Fuar*	Cold
		Fuaran	Spring of water
Ceann	Headland, high point	*Garbh, garve*	Rough
Clach	Stone	*Geodha*	Chasm
Clais	A hollow place	*Glas*	Green, sometimes grey
Cleit	A high rocky ridge		
Cnap, cnoc	A hillock	*Gleann, glen*	Narrow valley with high surrounding mountains
Coire, corry	A rocky cauldron in the mountains		
Creag	Rocky cliff	*Gualann*	Shoulder of the mountain
Dail	Wide valley		
Dearg	Red	*Lag*	Hollow place on a hillside
Drem, drom, drum, druim	High ridge, spine of a mountain		
		Lairig	Pass, or steep hillside
Dubh	Dark or black	*Leathad, leitir*	Slope
Dun	Fortification	*Leathan*	Broad
Each, eich	Horse	*Liath*	Grey

131

Lub	Curve
Machair	Low hills alongside the sea. Proverb: 'Fast walks the man of a thriftless wife along the machair of Uist'
Mam	Hill with gentle slopes
Maol	Bald hill, no vegetation
Meadhon	Central
Meall	Round hill
Monadh	Mountain
Mor, mhor, more	Great, big
Ord	Conical hill
Riabadh, riach	Drab grey
Roinn, Ros, Rhudha	Promontory
Ruigh	Shieling on sloping terrain
Sgeir	A rock surrounded by sea
Sgorr, sgurr	Conical peak
Sneachd	Snow
Sron	Naze
Stac, stuc	Pillar of steep rock
Stob	High point
Taigh, tigh	House
Teber, tobar	Spring of water
Tom, torr	Hillock
Tulach	High eminence in the hills
Uachdar, auchter	Uplands
Uamh	Cave
Uach	Steep declivity
Uisge	Water

Appendix 1

The Alpine Scene

All who are interested in mountains must be acquainted with the glamorous photographs of the Alpine regions of Switzerland, the Tirol, etc. These are exceptionally beautiful when the weather is as perfect as shown on the photographs, which is rare; but there are some drawbacks it is my duty to warn the beginner about.

A survey over the last ten years shows that Switzerland has in its mountain regions as much rain, mist and discomfort as Alaska or Wales in the worst winter. It is no joy either to reach the foot of the Matterhorn, and find a queue of forty parties waiting to go up, in one day. Charming as the views are when one can see them, Switzerland is wholly unsuitable for beginners because of the debatable technical value of the climbs.

Although Austria is slightly cheaper than Switzerland, so well named the millionaire's paradise, the entire Alpine region has more serious accidents than any other climbing area in the world, partly because the average climbs are to such heights that it is singularly difficult to get help to an injured man in time. Climbers in the Alpine region should take out insurance against accidents in their home country, because Swiss hospitals are notoriously expensive – so extortionate in fact that it is cheaper to be flown back home than stay in them.

As regards technique, Swiss and other Alpine heights are higher than many mountains elsewhere, but this does not always guarantee that they have climbs as exciting as those closer home. Height often means you spend a day climbing the foothills to get to the bottom of the ascent you really wish to make, which can be a source of boredom to a true enthusiast; and that day has to be paid for, since many interesting Swiss climbs are suicidal without a guide. No Alpine climbs should be composed of less than four people, which number is a fairly good maximum too. It is difficult not to be seduced by the attractive coloured photographs, especially those showing the convivial atmosphere of elegantly clad friends drinking together in the Alpine huts, but this is offset by the reality of the frequent stonefall avalanches (just of loose stones without any snow) all the year round, many of which are so considerable as to invalidate earlier maps, and by the fact that several Alpine surfaces are of flaked rock and very dangerous.

Climbs such as Green Death (X-severe), Oxford Street (in N. England), and various slopes in Scotland and Wales offer the most difficult climbing in the world from the technical point of view. (Green Death was made famous by Tom Proctor. This climb has almost no hold larger than the first joints of the fingers, is lichen-covered, and is wholly vertical.) In the Rocky Mountains, the Andes, the Drakensberg Mountains, the New Zealand Alps, Norway and the Pyrenees of Spain there are far better climbs than the Swiss can offer – except on tourist posters. For the truly adventurous, of course, there are the Himalayas or the heights of Africa, and the cost of getting there would hardly be more than a Swiss hotel bill.

Alpine climbs are carried on at heights not often encountered by many climbers, which means there is intense cold, and supplies have to be carried (including disinfectant, for some Alpine huts are not as clean as one would wish). Such climbs entail a larger rucksack, a heavier load, and a slower pace of progress than elsewhere. The unadvertised treachery of Alpine weather makes camping a dubious thing, except in the best months of the year, and this almost forces one to stop at the huts of the various Alpine clubs. Beginners should be warned that some Alpine clubs exist to promote travel to the Swiss or Austrian Alps; and it has not been unknown for officials of such clubs to be basking in the luxury hotels of the host country while their members endure the cold comforts of hovels on the slopes. Alas for human nature!

Special techniques have to be learnt for Alpine climbing, such as keeping away from the cornice, walking well below the line of its possible collapse over the cliff edge, and, more dismally, keeping in the shady side of a mountain to give oneself a clearer chance of escape from avalanches. In avalanche conditions one of the dangers is suffocation either from being buried in the snow, or because there is not enough oxygen amid the falling snow. In sunshine verglas may cause difficulties, making surfaces excessively slippery. It is best to have two or

Be diligent, work as part of a team, never take risks, and enjoy your climbing

three years' experience of long winter climbing holidays in your own country before venturing to climb in the European Alps.

Swiss guides are inclined to insist upon people buying local equipment, which can add to the expenses of a climber trying to feed himself in that playboys' country. Not that Swiss food is all that good. I suffered from food poisoning after a meal at a four-star hotel. Some Swiss hoteliers seem to rely upon exotic sauces to cloak the age and quality of the meat they serve up.

The Alpine regions have great beauty, and there are a few climbs, such as the Eiger North Wall, which attract the super-enthusiast. But even that is hardly more exciting than the 1,200ft (366m) North Wall of St John's Head, Hoy, which took two such experts as Edward Drummond and Oliver Hill seven days to ascend (1970). As for excitement, this outpost of the Orkneys is savaged by the weight of 3,000 miles (4,828km) of untamed Atlantic storms every day of the year.

Appendix 2

Mountain Photography

Firstly, it is important to know what you want your photographs for – as personal memories, and to share with friends and family, or as saleable products for magazines and newspapers. If personal memories are your aim, virtually any of the cheaper cameras will serve; but for transparencies and prints intended for sale, a much more expensive model will be required. A good camera may save you a dozen ascents in search of the perfect shot. Nikon, Leica, Contax and Asahi are excellent makes in the more expensive range, and currently the first named is much favoured by experts.

Secondly, the weight of photographic equipment to be carried must be estimated. I recall doing some mountaineering with a famous climber who was a most enthusiastic photographer, and he took no less than five cameras on each ascent, with extension tubes, telephoto lenses, etc. The snag in this was that he unselfishly shared out the burdens with those making the ascent with him, so that I usually ended up carrying two cameras, and whenever we were on some perilous crag, my friend would peremptorily demand one of his cameras for the shot of the century. I am now of the opinion that anybody who needs that much photographic gear should make the ascent by helicopter. Work out in advance what sort of photographs you wish to take, and you will find that it is seldom necessary to take up telephoto and wide-angle lenses, or cameras with different-speed films wound on, as my famous friend did.

If you know nothing about cameras, go and talk to a photographic dealer (one whose work is selling cameras and keeping his customers happy), and tell him what sort of photographs you want to take and what you can afford to spend. It is in his best interest to give you good advice, because then he can expect you to become a regular customer, buying films and having them printed at his establishment.

In the mountains the best seasons for photography are usually late spring and early autumn. Occasionally there are clear sunny days in winter, but summer is frequently cloudy or rainy in mountain country.

First attempts of mountain photography are sometimes not sharp enough to be wholly successful. Start with the lens at infinity, and then you can stop down to bring as much of the foreground into focus as you need. Autumn is, of course, the best time for colour photography on the lower slopes, where there is more vegetation.

If you want to include people as well as the scenery, you may do well to take a wide-angle lens. At least it avoids the need for asking friends to step backwards!

One of the snags of mountain photography is the greater likelihood of camera shake. Dangerous or difficult footholds, rope movements, or winds gusting suddenly can all produce an unsteadiness that would not occur down below. You can steady yourself either by leaning firmly back against a rock or kneeling or sitting. Film is costly, and mountaineering consumes energy and is often hazardous, so practise with your camera before you take it up.

For the less complicated cameras and black and white film (which often gives the most startling mountain shots) an aperture of F8 or F11 with a 1/250th second exposure is a fairly reliable average setting. Few people can hold a camera still longer than 1/30th second, but this is usually too slow for many mountain shots. If you use black and white film, add a filter. Ultra-violet filters greatly enhance the lighting effects found in the sky and yellow (No 2) filters improve the effects of clouds dramatically. If you wish to take shots of bare rock with no vegetation, depending on their shadows and such natural features as rain courses for contrast, you had better take up a pale orange filter.

If you camp in the mountains, rise early. You can get some remarkably beautiful photographs when, as Tennyson described the dawn,

> East and West, without a breath
> Mixt their dim lights, like Life and Death,
> To broaden into boundless day.

There are constant improvements in films, and it is as well to ask your local dealer which type of film he thinks fit, or prefers best, for mountain work. The type of film may also relate to the light in a particular season of the year. If in doubt, a letter to the main manufacturers will elicit good advice.

There is always surplus light in the mountains, and not only in the brilliant sunlit conditions in which you would expect it; those rock surfaces throw light about and reflect it in ways that are less apparent to the naked eye than to the camera lens. For that and other reasons it is a good idea to pack a lens hood with the camera; this device weighs virtually nothing, but excludes surplus light and gives a much improved clarity of picture.

Still some errors may occur, so let us look at the most common causes. It is very easy to take a light-meter reading, and then shift your position, perhaps just from one foot to the other, and the exact angle of the camera's relation to the light will be altered – and light angles are exact. Anyway, on a mountain it cannot be emphasised too strongly that neither the photographer nor anybody he is photographing should ever shift their position without first looking where hands and feet are going. I failed to heed this advice once, and once was enough. 'Could you step two paces back?' I was asked. I did, right up to my knees in a cottongrass bog!

Do not place your main subject in the dead centre of every picture, especially if your sweetheart has just climbed the highest she has ever climbed. Let others see a little bit of the mountain as well as your beloved. A balanced picture means one in which the contents do not cancel each other out. Try to compose your picture in your viewfinder (reflex cameras make this easier), and never rely upon editing or the cutting room to make your picture successful.

Interesting angles to look for are the shadows of clouds on rocks and in the valleys far below. There is also much charm in the different light angles created by water dripping over rocks, mosses, and so on.

Some backgrounds are inclined to be fussy, so try to cut the main subject out from the background, even if it means lying on your face or on your back to get an unusual angle. Do not forget that in black and white film numerous shades distinct to you may appear just as a vague grey backdrop.

I know from experience that often one sees the most tempting views on a freezing cold day, and the temptation is to risk the icy cold for what you believe is the Photo of the Year. The best advice I can give in those circumstances is that if you wish to take off your mitts and kneel on a lump of ice because the view is worth it to you, please try to do so on the way down. Should the after-effects upset you, you would then be in less trouble, being nearer home.

Unfortunately the weather in mountain terrain is continually changing, and the serious enthusiast may have to make several ascents to take the scene in the lighting he wants. That is always a good excuse to climb again, however.

Here are some simple reminders for those in a hurry:

1 *Focus.* The smaller the lens aperture, the greater the depth of field. Conversely, the larger the lens aperture, the less the depth of field. Depth of field is the really clear area on either side of the exact centre of the point of focus. We speak of F2, F2·8, F4, F8, F16, F22, etc. These numbers are very simple to understand: for example, F8 means that when the lens stop is adjusted to this number, the width of the aperture is one-eighth of the focal length (which separates the centre of the lens from the centre of the film) when the camera is focused on infinity.

2 *Speed of film.* The finer the grain structure visible on an enlarged picture, the slower the speed of the film used to take it. Conversely, fast film gives a coarser visible grain structure on any enlargement than slow film. Use fast film for photography in poor light. Remember that a faster film speed generally requires a smaller lens aperture. To improve your work consult *Practical Photography* by Arthur Nettleton (Foyles Handbook Series).

Frank Smythe said in *The Spirit of the Hills*: 'Mountaineering is a search for beauty. There is beauty all about us, and the more we develop our vision the more we perceive it. Beauty is as necessary to Man as food and drink.'

Bibliography

Alexander, H., Watson, A., *et al. The Cairngorms* (West Col, 1968)

Auden, W. H. and Isherwood, C. *The Ascent of F6* (Faber, 1958)

Bell, J. H. B. *A Progress in Mountaineering* (Oliver & Boyd, 1950)

Bell, J. H. B., Bozman, E. F. and Blakeborough, J. F. *British Hills and Mountains* (Batsford, 1940)

Bird, Vivian. *Bird's Eye View: the Midlands* (Roundwood Press, 1973)

Blackshaw, Alan. *Mountaineering* (Penguin, 1970)

Bonnington, Chris. *Annapurna, South Face* (Gollancz, 1969)

——. *I Chose to Climb* (Gollancz, 1966)

Borthwick, J. *Always a Little Further* (Smith, 1969)

Bridge, George. *Rock Climbing in the British Isles* (West Col, 1971) (a survey covering 1894–1970)

Brown, Joe. *The Hard Years* (Gollancz, 1967)

Byne, E. *High Peak* (Secker & Warburg, 1966)

Carr, Glyn. *Fat Man's Agony* (Collins, 1969) (a climbing whodunit?)

Clough, Ian. *Ben Nevis and Glencoe* (Cicerone Press, 1972)

Collumb, R. G. *Grampians East* (West Col, 1969)

Condry, William. *Exploring Wales* (Faber, 1970)

Cowley, Bill. *Cleveland Way* (Dalesman, 1975)

Crew, Peter. *Anglesey–Gogarth* (West Col, 1970)

——. *Encyclopaedic Dictionary of Mountaineering* (Constable, 1968)

The Dales Way (Ramblers' Association)

Disley, John. *Tackle Climbing This Way* (Stanley Paul, 1959)

Donaldson, J. C. and Coates, W. L. *Munro's Tables,* revised ed (West Col, 1969)

Evans, C. *On Climbing* (Museum Press, 1956)

Fedden, Robin. *The Enchanted Mountains* (J. Murray, 1962) (on the Pyrenees)

Firbank, Thomas. *I Bought a Mountain* (White Lion Publishers, 1972)

Frazer, Colin. *The Avalanche Enigma* (Murray, 1966)

Gray, Affleck. *The Big Grey Man of Ben Macdhui* (Impulse Books, 1970) (about the Scottish Yeti, ghostly voices and music)

Gray, Dennis. *Rope Boy* (Gollancz, 1970)

Greenbank, A. *Instructions in Rock Climbing* (Museum Press, 1963)

Bibliography

Griffin, A. H. *The Roof of England* (Hale, 1970)

Hassall, G. A. *The Northern Lake District* (Cicerone Press, 1969) (covers difficult–severe climbs)

Heaton-Cooper, W. *The Tarns of Lakeland* (H. Cooper Studio, 1970)

Herzog, Maurice. *Annapurna* (C. Chivers, 1974)

Hogan, J. M. *Impelled into Experience* (EP, 1968) (an Outward Bound book)

Howard, Tony. *Walks and Climbs in Romsdal* (Cicerone Press, 1970) (deals with Norway)

Hunt, John. *Ascent of Everest* (Hodder, 1953)

James, Ron. *Rock Climbing in Wales* (Constable, 1970)

Jones, Trevor. *Snowdon South* (Climbers' Club, 1970)

King, H. G. R. *The Antarctic* (Blandford Press, 1969)

Kirkus, C. F. *Let's Go Climbing* (Nelson, 1960)

Law, D. *Young Person's Nature Guide* (Gifford, 1972)

Marr, Anthony. *North York Moors* (West Col, 1970)

Marshall, J. R. *Ben Nevis* (West Col, 1969)

Meldrum, Kim and Royle, Brian. *Artificial Climbing Walls* (Pelham, 1970)

Merrill, J. N. *Walking in Derbyshire* (Dalesman, 1969)

Milne, M. *Book of Modern Mountaineering* (Barker, 1968)

Moffat, Gwen. *On My Home Ground* (Hodder, 1968)

Moulam, A. J. J. *Carneddau* (West Col, 1972)

——. *Cwm Idwal* (West Col, 1972)

Mountain Rescue (HMSO)

Mulgrew, P. *No Place for Men* (Kaye, 1965) (deals with New Zealand)

Mummery, A. F. *My Climbs in the Alps and Caucasus* (Blackwell, 1936)

Oldham, K. *Pennine Way* (Dalesman, 1972)

Poucher W. A. *Lakeland Peaks* (Constable, 1972)

——. *Peaks and Pennines* (Constable, 1966)

——. *Scottish Peaks* (Constable, 1964)

——. *Welsh Peaks* (Constable, 1962)

Pyatt, E. C. *A Climber in the West Country* (David & Charles, 1969)

——. *Climbing and Walking in S.E. England* (David & Charles, 1970)

Richard, Colette. *Climbing Blind* (Hodder, 1966) (the author is blind herself)

Roberts, David. *Mountain of My Fear* (Souvenir Press, 1969) (set in Alaska)

Scarr, J. *Four Miles High* (Gollancz, 1966)

Shipton, Eric. *That Untravelled World* (Hodder, 1969)

Simpson, Myrtle. *White Horizons* (Gollancz, 1967) (deals with Greenland)

Slessor, M. *The Andes are Prickly* (Gollancz, 1966)

Smythe, Frank. *Adventure of a Mountaineer* (Hodder, 1935)

——. *The Spirit of the Hills* (Hodder, 1946)

——. *The Valley of Flowers* (Hodder, 1935)

Spencer Chapman, Freddy. *Memoirs of a Mountaineer* (Reprint Society, 1945)

142

Steven, Campbell R. *The Central Highlands* (West Col, 1968)

Talbot, J. O. *Gower Peninsula* (West Col, 1970)

Ullman, J. R. *Americans on Everest* (Michael Joseph, 1966)

Unsworth, W. *Book of Rock Climbing* (Barker, 1968)

Wainwright, A. *Pennine Way Companion* (Westmorland Gazette, 1968)

——. *Walks in Limestone Country* (Westmorland Gazette, 1970)

Wallace, W. M. M. *Climbers' Guide to Arran* (West Col, 1970)

Ward, M. *The Mountaineer's Companion* (Eyre & Spottiswoode, 1966)

Whymper, Edward. *Great Andes of the Equator* (Knight, 1972)

——. *Scrambles amongst the Alps* (Murray, 1954)

Young, G. Winthrop. *Mountain Craft* (Methuen, 1949)

——. *On High Hills* (Methuen, 1947)